COSMIC COMBINATIONS

A Book of Astrological Exercises

By Joan Negus

Published by
Astro Computing Services
PO Box 16430
San Diego, CA 92116

Distributed by
Para Research, Inc.
Whistlestop Mall
Rockport, MA 01966

Other books by JOAN NEGUS
Basic Astrology: A Guide for Teachers and Students
Basic Astrology: A workbook for Students

Also published by ASTRO COMPUTING SERVICES
The American Atlas
The American Book of Tables
The American Ephemeris for the 20th Century [Midnight]
The American Ephemeris for the 20th Century [Noon]
The American Ephemeris for the 21st Century
The American Ephemeris 1901 to 1930
The American Ephemeris 1931 to 1980 & Book of Tables
The American Ephemeris 1941 to 1950
The American Ephemeris 1951 to 1960
The American Ephemeris 1961 to 1970
The American Ephemeris 1971 to 1980
The American Ephemeris 1981 to 1990
The American Ephemeris 1991 to 2000
The American Sidereal Ephemeris 1976 to 2000
The American Heliocentric Ephemeris 1901 to 2000
Interpreting the Eclipses (Jansky)
The American Book of Charts (Rodden)
Astrological Insights Into Personality (Lundsted)
The Fortunes of Astrology (Granite)
Planetary Planting (Riotte)
Planting by the Moon (Best & Kollerstrom)
The Only Way to...Learn Astrology, Vol. I
Basic Principles (March & McEvers)
The Only Way to...Learn Astrology, Vol. II
Math & Interpretation Techniques (March & McEvers)
The Lively Circle (Koval)

Copyright © 1982 by Joan Negus
All rights reserved. No part of this book may be reproduced or used in any form or by any means — graphic, electronic or mechanical, including photocopying, mimeographing, recording, taping or information storage and retrieval systems — without written permission from the publisher. A reviewer may quote brief passages.

International Standard Book Number 0-917086-37-6
Printed by Hamilton Printing Company

TABLE OF CONTENTS

Introduction..i

EXERCISES
1. Triplicities, Quadruplicities, Polarity...................1
2. Symbols and Rulerships................................2
3. Aries...3
4. Taurus...4
5. Gemini...5
6. Cancer...6
7. Leo..7
8. Virgo..8
9. Libra..9
10. Scorpio...10
11. Sagittarius...11
12. Capricorn...12
13. Aquarius..13
14. Pisces..14
15. Sign Combinations 1..................................15
16. Sign Combinations 2..................................16
17. Sign Combinations 3..................................17
18. Sign Combinations 4..................................18
19. Sign Combinations 5..................................19
20. Sign Combinations 6..................................20
21. Sign Combinations 7..................................21
22. Sign Combinations 8..................................22
23. Sign Combinations 9..................................23
24. Sign Combinations 10.................................24
25. Sign Combinations 11.................................25
26. Sign Combinations 12.................................26
27. Houses..27
28. Signs in Houses 1....................................28
29. Signs in Houses 2....................................29
30. Signs in Houses 3....................................30
31. Signs in Houses 4....................................31
32. Signs in Houses 5....................................32
33. Signs in Houses 6....................................33
34. Signs in Houses 7....................................34
35. Signs in Houses 8....................................35
36. Signs in Houses 9....................................36
37. Signs in Houses 10...................................37
38. Planets...38

39. Planets in Houses 1	39
40. Planets in Houses 2	40
41. Planets in Houses 3	41
42. Planets in Houses 4	42
43. Planets in Houses 5	43
44. Planets in Houses 6	44
45. Planets in Houses 7	45
46. Planets in Houses 8	46
47. Planets, Signs, Houses 1	47
48. Planets, Signs, Houses 2	48
49. Planets, Signs, Houses 3	49
50. Planets, Signs, Houses 4	50
51. Planets, Signs, Houses 5	51
52. Planets, Signs, Houses 6	52
53. Planets, Signs, Houses 7	53
54. Planets, Signs, Houses 8	54
Introduction to Exercises 55-58	55
55. Planets in Aspect 1	56
56. Planets in Aspect 2	57
57. Planets in Aspect 3	58
58. Planets in Aspect 4	59
Introduction to Nodes	60
59. Nodes in Aspect	61
60. MC in Aspect	62
61. Ascendant in Aspect	63
62. Major Configurations 1	64
63. Major Configurations 2	65
64. Major Configurations 3	66
65. Major Configurations 4	67
66. Major Configurations 5	68
Introduction to Chart Interpretation	69
67. Chart Interpretation 1	84
68. Chart Interpretation 2	85
69. Chart Interpretation 3	86
70. Chart Interpretation 4	87
71. Chart Interpretation 5	89
72. Chart Interpretation 6	90
73. Chart Interpretation 7	92
74. Chart Interpretation 8	94
75. Chart Interpretation 9	96

76. Martin Luther King..................................100
77. King's Configurations.............................101
78. King's Career 1......................................102
79. King's Career 2......................................102
80. King's Partnerships 1..............................103
81. King's Partnerships 2..............................103
82. King's Communications 1.........................104
83. King's Communications 2.........................104
84. Eleanor Roosevelt..................................107
85. Roosevelt's Configurations.......................108
86. Roosevelt's Distant Travel 1.....................109
87. Roosevelt's Distant Travel 2.....................109
88. Roosevelt's Publishing 1..........................110
89. Roosevelt's Publishing 2..........................110
90. Roosevelt's Partnerships 1.......................111
91. Roosevelt's Partnerships 2.......................111
92. Babe Ruth..114
93. Ruth's Configurations..............................115
94. Ruth's Athletics 1...................................116
95. Ruth's Athletics 2...................................116
96. Ruth's Group Involvement 1......................117
97. Ruth's Group Involvement 2......................117
98. Ruth's Partnerships 1..............................118
99. Ruth's Partnerships 2..............................118

ANSWERS..119
Bibliography..155
Birth Source Information...............................155

DEDICATION
To the twenty students who participated in this project, and whose support and critcism helped me to shape the exercises into their final form.

INTRODUCTION

The interpretation of a horoscope requires more than the mere dissection of its details. It represents a total being, greater than the sum of its parts. Delineation is thus a synthesizing process that entails integrating key words for signs, planets, houses and aspects in order to describe a whole person.

Many introductory astrology texts offer adequate sections on the individual astrological factors, but once these facts are presented, the student is left to his own devices to synthesize; or the teacher assumes the task. Studying the basics is relatively simple in that one learns each planet, sign, house and aspect separately, but the integration that follows can seem confusing and endless. The exercises in this book were created to offer an orderly way to master a vast and complex area that is nevertheless essential to successful chart interpretation.

The definitions given in this book are by no means all-inclusive. Each one is a possibility that can be a springboard to stimulate the student to develop skills further and to expand the knowledge needed for the art of delineation. The exercises have been tested by a large number of students in classroom situations and used in conjunction with interpretation of actual charts. By actively participating in this process (as opposed to a teacher giving a monologue), learning became a valuable joint effort.

The answers given often trigger such statements as 'But I read in a book that Venus connected with Saturn also means...' or 'I have that combination in my chart and it has manifested in this way....' Such sharing of experience speeds the understanding of the astrological principles. For the student using the book alone, on the other hand, the exercises offer a frame of reference for organizing material gleaned from other sources. This book does not replace an introductory course, but it can supplement it substantially. Presentation of the meanings of signs, planets, houses and aspects should precede it; and a systematic method of chart interpretation should accompany it. There are a number of ways to delineate a horoscope and these exercises can be coordinated with any approach that begins with a holistic view of the chart, and proceeds to the individual details. The following is only one such system.*

A worksheet including most of the material given below can be found on p. 53 of my book *Basic Astrology: A Guide for Teachers and Students,* and p. 29 of *Basic Astrology: A Workbook*

i

for Students. If *Basic Astrology* is used as the basis for the introductory material, the exercises in this book should be commenced after the major configurations have been presented.

Every horoscope contains all twelve signs of the zodiac, and the same ten planets and twelve houses, but the manner in which they are combined varies according to date, time and place of birth. Each of the 34 primary factors in astrology has its own basic qualities, but it is the combination of factors that makes the individual unique. Some signs are more strongly emphasized than others in a given horoscope, thus making the characteristics of those signs more evident than others. The planets, which denote energies or functions, are influenced by sign and house placement. And the areas of life, indicated by the houses, are described by the signs and planets in the house and planets connected with them.

Since the signs are the broadest of the three categories given above, it is best to start the overview of the chart with examination of them. Sign emphasis is shown by: (1) position of the Sun, Moon and Ascendant; (2) stelliums (three or more planets or points) in a sign; (3) stelliums in a house (houses are related to the signs of the natural zodiac so that, for example, a first house stellium would indicate an Aries emphasis); and (4) a count of planets in triplicities and quadruplicities by sign and house. Each sign has a mode and element with no combination being repeated (Aries is the cardinal-fire sign, Leo the fixed-fire sign, Sagittarius the mutable-fire sign, etc.). The highest count by element and mode represents the emphasis of a particular sign.

The count of planets by element and mode also reveals important general traits even before you discover the highest number of each to show a sign emphasis. A person with a majority of planets in fire has enthusiasm and zeal. An earth person is practical and likes to deal with tangibles, but may be limited to material and physical considerations. An air person handles ideas and abstractions well, likes to communicate, but without the help of other elements may be inclined to rationalize. A water person is sympathetic and intuitive but may be ruled by uncontrolled feelings. An individual with a cardinal emphasis will probably be an initiator and likes to be 'where the action is.' A fixed individual resists change, is persistent, and usually goal-oriented. And a mutable individual will be flexible and adaptable, but perhaps indecisive.

Once sign emphasis is determined by planets in signs and houses, major configurations (T-Squares, Grand Crosses, Grand Trines, Cradles and Yods) should be examined and added to the data. These multiple aspects mark repeated patterns in the native's life. First note the quality of the configurations. T-Squares and Grand Crosses are hard. They indicate conflicts that must be resolved (squares) and balanced (oppositions). Since T-Squares and Grand Crosses involve planets or points in square to each other, they are usually in the same mode (cardinal, fixed or mutable); and the mode indicates how problems will manifest themselves. If the configuration is in cardinal signs, action is the key word—one involves oneself in situations and tries to cope with them by attempting various solutions that deal with them directly. If fixed, particular problems will be repeated and the means of trying to solve them will likewise be similar. If mutable, other persons are usually involved in the problem, and one may flounder from solution to solution.

Grand Trines indicate what flows easily, and since the planets and points are in trine to each other they will usually be in the same element. The element indicates the way the 'flow' is manifested—through zeal and enthusiasm if fire; through practicality if earth; through abstractions, communications and other mental functions if air; and through intuition and emotions if water. Cradles (four or more planets or points connected by sextiles, with the first and last factors usually forming an opposition) denote help from others. Yods (two planets or points sextile each other and both quincunx a third planet or point) depict a crucial change at some time in the native's life, although this change is usually not self-initiated.

The particular planets and points in the configuration show more definitely the types of problems or assets which the individual may have. For instance, if one has a T-Square involving Mercury, Saturn and Uranus there will probably be problems to be resolved in terms of communications. Communications may be erratic or stilted. If the T-Square is in cardinal signs, one may alternate between 'putting one's foot in one's mouth' and keeping silent too long. When the potential problem is recognized one can work toward using the positive energies of the planets—put thoughts (Mercury) in order (Saturn) and then speak (Mercury) with originality (Uranus). Any sextiles or trines connected with the planets or points offer ways one can easily begin to activiate the pattern positively. If the Sun trines Saturn one might consider, for example, ego needs while putting thoughts in order.

Grand Trines should be investigated in like manner, although they represent energies that flow easily. Since obstacles are not involved, the result may be some kind of excess. If one has a Grand Trine in fire involving Jupiter, Mars and

Venus, one may enthusiastically (fire) initiate (Mars) on a large scale (Jupiter) and receive pleasure (Venus) doing so. Or one may enthusiastically (fire) undertake (Mars) too many (Jupiter) pleasurable (Venus) projects. Look for squares and oppositions to the planets to discipline and direct the energies.

Further clues to life patterns are provided by the house placement of the planets involved and the houses ruled by these planets. These indicate areas where the energies will most likely emerge. Once the overall picture of the individual is formed, any area of the native's life may be examined. Determine the house that represents the area to be investigated and proceed from the most general requirements to the specific. The sign or signs within the house indicate the basic needs in the area. For example, if the area of the home (fourth house) is being studied, and this house contains the signs of Sagittarius and Capricorn, the individual will need a home in which there is flexibility, where he can grow and develop (Sagittarius); but also a place with security, stability and order (Capricorn).

If there are any planets in the house the requirements become more specific. Any aspects to these planets will show whether these needs are fulfilled easily or with effort. Venus in the fourth house would probably indicate that the native needs beauty in the home. If Venus were square Neptune this might mean that there could be disappointment with the results of efforts to fulfill this need. Perhaps he or she could learn to use more intuition and sensitivity (Neptune) in decorating the home. If Venus were also part of a major configuration, situations that might arise in this area would have more facets.

The planet that rules the house being studied further expands the description of that area. The house position of the ruler shows a connection between that house and the area being investigated. If the ruler of the fourth house is in the tenth, the native might work from the home or bring his work into the home. Single aspects and major configurations involving the ruler can further broaden the picture of the area being examined.

There are other factors that can be noted for a more detailed interpretation. It is important to look for the reinforcement of repeated messages in the chart. This is done to some extent by observing the signs that are emphasized repeatedly. Factors other than signs should, however, be considered in a thorough delineation. For instance, initiative or aggressiveness may be indicated by the sign Aries, by a predominantly eastern chart (a majority of the planets on the left of the MC-IC axis) and/or by a prominently placed Mars.

A systematic method of interpreting a chart, such as the above, gives the exercises in this book a framework. The exercises, as previously stated, are intended to assist in the process of integration. They begin with examination of the signs and increase in complexity to combinations of two signs, then three. Houses are presented next, followed by signs in houses. Planets come next; then planets in signs, planets in signs and houses and planets in aspect. And finally, in this first section, major configurations are introduced. The rest of the book is devoted to applying the principles presented in the first part to interpreting charts. As the student thinks more and more in terms of combinations, facility in chart delineation will result.

EXERCISE 1 Triplicities, Quadruplicities, Polarity

Each sign of the zodiac has definite characteristics that differentiate it from the other signs, but each shares some qualities with certain other signs by virtue of quadruplicity (element), triplicity (mode), and polarity. Place the appropriate letter next to each definition given below.

a. Fire signs— ♈ ♌ ♐   e. Cardinal signs— ♈ ♋ ♎ ♑
b. Earth signs—♉ ♍ ♑   f. Fixed signs— ♉ ♌ ♏ ♒
c. Air signs— ♊ ♎ ♒   g. Mutable signs—♊ ♍ ♐ ♓
d. Water signs—♋ ♏ ♓   h. Positive signs (+)—♈ ♊ ♌ ♎ ♐ ♒
                       i. Negative signs (-)— ♉ ♋ ♍ ♏ ♑ ♓

Which signs are:
1. Extroverted? _____
2. Emotional and intuitive? _____
3. Initiating, and interested in being directly involved in situations? _____
4. Practical? _____
5. Interested in communications and can deal well with abstract ideas? _____
6. Introverted? _____
7. Flexible and adaptable? _____
8. Zealous, warm and enthusiastic? _____
9. Persistent or stubborn? _____

EXERCISE 2　　　　　　　　Symbols and Rulerships

Each sign has a connection with a house which can provide insights into the characteristics of the sign. If one starts with the sign of Aries (the first sign of the zodiac) and the first house, the correlation is simple to determine (Aries,1; Taurus,2; etc.)

Every sign has a symbol and a ruler or co-rulers, as well. The purpose of this exercise is to teach the symbol and ruler or co-rulers.

Place the appropriate number of the sign next to the symbols and rulers given below.

1. ♈
2. ♉
3. ♊
4. ♋
5. ♌
6. ♍

7. ♎
8. ♏
9. ♐
10. ♑
11. ♒
12. ♓

I. Symbols:

a. the Twins _____
b. the Ram _____
c. Fish _____
d. Scales _____
e. the Virgin _____
f. the Centaur _____

g. the Bull _____
h. the Mountain Goat _____
i. the Crab _____
j. the Water Bearer _____
k. the Lion _____
l. the Scorpion _____

II. Rulers (there may be more than one answer):

a. ☿ _____
b. ♆ ♃ _____
c. ☽ _____
d. ♂ _____
e. ♀ * ♂ _____

f. ♅ ♄ _____
g. ♀ _____
h. ☉ _____
i. ♄ _____
j. ♃ _____

* ♀ is also written sometimes as ♇.

EXERCISE 3   Aries

Aries ♈ : fire—enthusiasm and zeal; cardinal—initiating and actively engaged; positive—extroverted; symbol—the Ram, which elicits the idea of pushing forward without thought of the consequences; house connection—1, the me-first house, therefore, Aries is the me-first sign; ruler—Mars, the planet of initiative and aggression.

    Key words: Self-assertion, aggressiveness, zeal, self-centeredness, impatience, extroversion, quick responsiveness, initiative.

    When combined with other signs the qualities of Aries will be supported, modified or directed according to the characteristics of the other sign or signs involved. Place the appropriate letter or letters next to each question given below. Most of these will have more than one possible answer.

a. ♉
b. ♊
c. ♋
d. ♌
e. ♍
f. ♎

g. ♏
h. ♐
i. ♑
j. ♒
k. ♓

Which sign or signs might make Aries:

  1. Less self-centered and more motherly? _____

  2. More extroverted? _____

  3. Discipline the need for immediate gratification? _____

  4. Less aggressive? _____

  5. More enthusiastic and zealous? _____

  6. Channel its quickness into communications? _____

  7. More patient in dealing with details? _____

  8. Less self-assertive and more assertive for others? _____

  9. Initiating career-wise? _____

10. Less self-centered and more compassionate? _____

EXERCISE 4   Taurus

Taurus ♉ : earth—practical; fixed—persistent; negative—introverted; symbol—the Bull, which elicits the idea of steadfastness, perseverance and stubbornness; house connection—2, the house of one's own material resources, therefore, Taurus is interested in acquiring possessions; ruler—Venus, which introduces the idea of pleasure and art (but art that is functional or utilitarian, i.e., crafts).

Key words: Practicality, persistence, stubbornness, loyalty or steadfastness, possessiveness, sensuality, artistry.

When combined with other signs the qualities of Taurus will be supported, modified or directed according to the characteristics of the other sign or signs involved. Place the appropriate letter or letters next to each question given below. Most of these will have more than one possible answer.

a. ♈
b. ♊
c. ♋
d. ♌
e. ♍
f. ♎

g. ♏
h. ♐
i. ♑
j. ♒
k. ♓

Which sign or signs might make Taurus:
1. More persistent or stubborn? _____
2. Less stubborn and more adaptable? _____
3. Even more practical? _____
4. Focus the need for material possessions in the home? _____
5. Direct its loyalty toward a partner? _____
6. Even more possessive? _____
7. Temper its practicality with emotionality? _____
8. Apply its persistence to pursuing a career in acting? _____
9. Less cool and contained and more enthusiastic and zealous? _____
10. More gregarious? _____

EXERCISE 5 — Gemini

Gemini ♊: air—mental and communicative; mutable—adaptable and flexible; positive—extroverted; symbol—the Twins, which indicate diversity and duality; house connection—3, the house of communications and short journeys; ruler—Mercury, the planet of communication and manual dexterity.

Key words: adaptability, flexibility, fluctuation, gregariousness, mental agility, articulateness, duality, sociability.

When combined with other signs the qualities of Gemini will be supported, modified or directed according to the characteristics of the other sign or signs involved. Place the appropriate letter or letters next to each question given below. Most of these will have more than one possible answer.

a. ♈
b. ♉
c. ♋
d. ♌
e. ♍
f. ♎
g. ♏
h. ♐
i. ♑
j. ♒
k. ♓

Which sign or signs might make Gemini:

1. Less fluctuating and more persistent? _____
2. More flexible and adaptable? _____
3. More gregarious toward peer groups? _____
4. Use its mental agility in philosophy? _____
5. Communicate with enthusiasm and zeal? _____
6. Less flighty and more practical? _____
7. Combine emotional involvement with its sociability? _____
8. Enjoy communicating on a one-to-one basis? _____
9. Direct its mental agility toward analytical research? _____
10. Quick to articulate? _____

EXERCISE 6   Cancer

Cancer ♋: water—emotional and intuitive; cardinal—actively engaged (when home and family are involved); negative—introverted; symbol—the Crab, which has a hard shell to protect its tender flesh, denoting the vulnerability of the Cancerian and the ability to put on a facade to protect itself; house connection—4, the house of the home; ruler—the Moon, which shows the responsive and mothering qualities, as well as possible moodiness.

Key words: Motherliness, protectiveness, self-protectiveness, sensitivity, moodiness, deep emotionality, intuitiveness, home-orientation.

When combined with other signs the qualities of Cancer will be supported, modified or directed according to the characteristics of the other sign or signs involved. Place the appropriate letter or letters next to each question given below. Most of these will have more than one possible answer.

a. ♈
b. ♉
c. ♊
d. ♌
e. ♍
f. ♎

g. ♏
h. ♐
i. ♑
j. ♒
k. ♓

Which sign or signs might make Cancer:

1. Temper its emotionality with practicality? _____
2. Even more emotional and intuitive? _____
3. Less a "homebody" and more of a world-traveler? _____
4. Articulate its sensitivity? _____
5. Aggressively protect others? _____
6. Add warmth and enthusiasm to its mothering? _____
7. A meticulous home-maker? _____
8. Direct its mothering toward a partner? _____
9. Less moody and introverted and more outgoing? _____
10. Most sensitive to humanitarian causes? _____

EXERCISE 7   Leo

Leo ♌: fire—enthusiasm and zeal; fixed—persistent and stubborn; positive—extroverted; symbol—the Lion, the king of the jungle who enjoys begin the center of attention (therefore, the sign of the king or the actor); house connection—5, the house of creativity and procreation; ruler—the Sun, which elicits the idea of warmth and creativity.

Key words: Warm-heartedness, generosity, magnanimity, pomposity, dominating or domineering tendencies, creativeness.

When combined with other signs the qualities of Leo will be supported, modified or directed according to the characteristics of the other sign or signs involved. Place the appropriate letter or letters next to each question given below. Most of these will have more than one possible answer.

a. ♈
b. ♉
c. ♊
d. ♋
e. ♍
f. ♎
g. ♏
h. ♐
i. ♑
j. ♒
k. ♓

Which sign or signs might make Leo:

1. Keep its generosity within bounds? _____
2. Temper its pomposity with humility? _____
3. Less fixed and more pliable? _____
4. Even more zealous? _____
5. Less domineering and more willing to consider others as equals? _____
6. Even more stubborn? _____
7. Direct its warm-heartedness toward mothering? _____
8. Share the stage with a partner? _____
9. Add emotionality to its theatrical ability? _____
10 Less outgoing? _____

EXERCISE 8   Virgo

Virgo ♍: earth—practical; mutable—adaptable; negative—introverted; symbol—the Virgin, which brings to mind chastity and cleanliness; house connection— 6, the house of service, work and health; ruler— Mercury, mental activity and practical communications.

Key words: industriousness, devotedness to service, analytical and critical tendencies, interest in health and hygiene, hypochondria, detail-orientation, fussiness, meticulousness.

When combined with other signs the qualities of Virgo will be supported, modified or directed according to the characteristics of the other sign or signs involved. Place the appropriate letter or letters next to each question given below. Most of these will have more than one possible answer.

a. ♈
b. ♉
c. ♊
d. ♋
e. ♌
f. ♎
g. ♏
h. ♐
i. ♑
j. ♒
k. ♓

Which signs or signs might make Virgo:

1. Combine its service-orientation with self-sacrifice? _____
2. Even more practical? _____
3. Use its critical ability in being a critic for a newspaper? _____
4. Focus its interest in health and hygiene in foreign countries? _____
5. Add zeal to its industriousness? _____
6. Deep and probing in its analytical ability? _____
7. Utilize its detail-orientation in fine arts? _____
8. Direct its devotion to service toward humanitarian causes? _____
9. A meticulous housekeeper? _____
10. Less mutable and more persistent? _____

EXERCISE 9   Libra

Libra ♎: air—mental and communicative; cardinal—actively engaged (when partnership is involved); positive—extroverted; symbol—the Scales, which signifies the need for Libra to balance, and symbolizes fair-mindedness and possible indecisiveness; house connection—7, the house of partnership; ruler—Venus, denoting art (aesthetics and fine arts) and beauty (involving balance and harmony), and possible laziness.

Key words: Harmony, partnership, marriage, artistic and aesthetic values, diplomacy, tact, indolence, indecisiveness, balancing.

When combined with other signs the qualities of Libra will be supported, modified or directed according to the characteristics of the other sign or signs involved. Place the appropriate letter or letters next to each question given below. Most of these will have more than one possible answer.

a. ♈
b. ♉
c. ♊
d. ♋
e. ♌
f. ♍

g. ♏
h. ♐
i. ♑
j. ♒
k. ♓

Which sign or signs might make Libra:

1. More decisive? _____
2. Utilize diplomacy and tact in foreign affairs? _____
3. Less indolent and more ambitious? _____
4. Wish to be surrounded by beauty in the home? _____
5. Use its artistic ability for crafts? _____
6. Add enthusiasm and zeal to its calm demeanor? _____
7. Temper its aesthetic values with practicality? _____
8. Less airy and more emotional? _____
9. Tactful with peers? _____
10. Use its artistic ability in writing? _____

EXERCISE 10　　　　　　　　　　　　　　　　　　**Scorpio**

Scorpio ♏: water—emotional and intuitive; fixed—persistent and stubborn; negative—introverted; symbol—the Scorpion, thus Scorpios can "sting" and be formidable adversaries; house connection—8, the deep-probing house of birth, death, sex, regeneration and other people's resources; co-rulers—Mars, which forges ahead (in one direction with Scorpio) and Pluto, the deep- probing planet.

　　Key words: Emotional intensity, hard-driving and persistent aggressiveness, loyalty, pessimism; preoccupation with sex, death and regeneration; possessiveness, secretiveness, probing, penetration.

　　When combined with other signs the qualities of Scorpio will be supported, modified or directed according to the characteristics of the other sign or signs involved. Place the appropriate letter or letters next to each question given below. Most of these will have more than one possible answer.

a. ♈　　　　　　　g. ♎
b. ♉　　　　　　　h. ♐
c. ♊　　　　　　　i. ♑
d. ♋　　　　　　　j. ♒
e. ♌　　　　　　　k. ♓
f. ♍

Which signs or signs might make Scorpio:
1. Hard-driving career-wise? _____
2. Less secretive and more outgoing? _____
3. Utilize its deep-probing and penetrating ability in analytical research? _____
4. Less pessimistic? _____
5. Aggressive in the home? _____
6. Even more emotional? _____
7. Use other people's resources practically? _____
8. Incorporate its interest in sex, death and regeneration into a philosophy of life? _____
9. More communicative and less secretive? _____
10. Direct its loyalty toward a partner? _____

EXERCISE 11   Sagittarius

Sagittarius ♐: fire—enthusiasm and zeal; mutable—adaptable and flexible; positive—extroverted and outgoing; symbol—the Centaur shooting an arrow into space, elicitating the idea of broadening oneself through travel and knowledge; house connection—9, house of philosophy, religion, higher education and distant travel; ruler—Jupiter, the planet of optimism, growth and development.

    Key words: wanderlust, philosophy, mental growth and development, athletic inclinations, optimism, conviviality, outspokenness, enthusiasm.

    When combined with other signs the qualities of Sagittarius will be supported, modified or directed according to the characteristics of the other sign or signs involved. Place the appropriate letter or letters next to each question given below. Most of these will have more than one possible answer.

a. ♈
b. ♉
c. ♊
d. ♋
e. ♌
f. ♍
g. ♎
h. ♏
i. ♑
j. ♒
k. ♓

Which sign or signs might make Sagittarius:

1. Limit its urge for distant travel because of attachment to the home? _____
2. Direct its philosophical interests toward mysticism? _____
3. Even more enthusiastic? _____
4. Use its athletic inclinations in a team effort? _____
5. Less outspoken and more introverted? _____
6. Enjoy short trips as well as distant travel? _____
7. Share its philosophical ideas with a partner? _____
8. Temper its outspokenness for practical reasons? _____
9. Grow and develop through serving others? _____
10. Less optimistic? _____

EXERCISE 12   Capricorn

Capricorn ♑ : earth—practical; cardinal—actively engaged (regarding one's role in the world); negative—introverted; symbol—the Mountain Goat, persistent and steadfast climber; house connection—10, the house of career and one's role in the outer world, therefore symbolizing career emphasis and ambition; ruler—Saturn, goal-orientation, discipline and seriousness.

Key words: ambition, patience, convention, conservatism, tradition, status-seeking, discipline, strong sense of duty, unrelenting climber.

When combined with other signs the qualities of Capricorn will be supported, modified or directed according to the characteristics of the other sign or signs involved. Place the appropriate letter or letters next to each question given below. Most of these will have more than one possible answer.

a. ♈
b. ♉
c. ♊
d. ♋
e. ♌
f. ♍
g. ♎
h. ♏
i. ♐
j. ♒
k. ♓

Which sign or signs might make Capricorn:

1. Temper its ambition with compassion for others? _____
2. Less conventional and traditional? _____
3. Direct its strong sense of duty toward a partner? _____
4. Even more persistent? _____
5. Less patient? _____
6. Use its discipline in writing? _____
7. Less conservative and more outgoing? _____
8. Add emotionality to its practicality? _____
9. Use its ambition and persistence to pursue a career in acting? _____
10. Seek status in a foreign country? _____

EXERCISE 13   Aquarius

Aquarius ♒: Air—mental and communicative; fixed— determined and persistent; positive—extroverted; symbol—the Water Bearer (carrying words or wisdom); house connection—11, the house of equality, peers, organizations, hopes and wishes (ideals); co-rulers—Saturn, indicating an interest in social structure and the world-at-large, and Uranus, the planet of independence, individuality and revolutionary tendencies.

Key words: humanitarian idealism, impersonal detachment, urge to liberate or be liberated, non-conformity, egalitarianism, revolution.

When combined with other signs the qualities of Aquarius will be supported, modified or directed according to the characteristics of the other sign or signs involved. Place the appropriate letter or letters next to each question given below. Most of these will have more than one possible answer.

a. ♈
b. ♉
c. ♊
d. ♋
e. ♌
f. ♍
g. ♎
h. ♏
i. ♐
j. ♑
k. ♓

Which sign or signs might make Aquarius:

1. Less impersonal and more emotionally involved? _____

2. Even more intellectual? _____

3. More conservative and less liberal? _____

4. Take initiative in revolutionary uprisings? _____

5. Direct its humanitarian idealism toward foreign causes? _____

6. Enjoy performing before groups on the stage? _____

7. Temper its non-conformity to obtain goals? _____

8. Combine its egalitarianism with fair-mindedness? _____

9. Add enthusiasm and zeal to its ability to communicate? _____

10. Need a great deal of freedom in the home? _____

EXERCISE 14   Pisces

Pisces ♓: water—emotional and intuitive; mutable—adaptable and flexible; negative—introverted; symbol—the Fish, symbolizing elusiveness; house connection—12, the house of mysticism, spirituality, the subconscious and unconscious mind; co-rulers—Jupiter, the planet of growth (in the spiritual sense) and Neptune, signifying nebulousness, imagination, spirituality, illusion, delusion, self-sacrifice.

    Key words: Compassion, empathy, self-sacrifice, intuitiveness, mysticism, spiritualism, nebulousness, vulnerability to delusion and/or victimization.

    When combined with other signs the qualities of Pisces will be supported, modified or directed according to the characteristics of other sign or signs involved. Place the appropriate letter or letters next to each question given below. Most of these will have more than one possible answer.

a. ♈
b. ♉
c. ♊
d. ♋
e. ♌
f. ♍
g. ♎
h. ♏
i. ♐
j. ♑
k. ♒

Which signs or signs might make Pisces:

1. Even more intuitive? _____
2. Less nebulous and more practical? _____
3. Combine spiritualism with philosophy? _____
4. More aggressive and less reticent? _____
5. Self-sacrificing toward a partner? _____
6. Use its compassion in humanitarian causes? _____
7. Pursue mysticism with zeal and enthusiasm? _____
8. Use its imaginative ability in communications? _____
9. Even more flexible and adaptable? _____
10. An empathetic actor? _____

EXERCISE 15 — Sign Combinations 1

The purpose of this group of exercises is to help the student integrate the characteristics of three signs. The descriptions isolate one possible key word for each sign involved, but there are other probable manifestations of the same combination.
Place the most appropriate letter next to each description.

a. ♈ ♋ ♑
b. ♈ ♏ ♐
c. ♌ ♍ ♎
d. ♊ ♑ ♒

e. ♉ ♍ ♓
f. ♌ ♒ ♓
g. ♉ ♊ ♐
h. ♋ ♎ ♏

1. An individual who might combine acting ability with deep emotion and enjoy performing before groups. _____
2. A person who would be ambitious and has energetic initiative but is very much attached to his home. _____
3. An individual who could be a world traveler and write about his experiences in a practical way. _____
4. Someone who is motherly toward a partner but also needs time to be alone. _____
5. A person who might be an artist with a dramatic flare but yet is interested in detail. _____
6. Somebody who could be outgoing and philosophical but also deep-probing and emotional. _____
7. A person who might display executive ability on the social scene or in humanitarian causes. _____
8. One who would be self-sacrificing and service-oriented but only so long as he receives material rewards. _____

EXERCISE 16   Sign Combinations 2

The purpose of this group of exercises is to help the student integrate the characteristics of three signs. The descriptions isolate one possible key word for each sign involved, but there are other probable manifestations of the same combination.
Place the most appropriate letter next to each description.

a. ♈ ♊ ♌
b. ♌ ♎ ♐
c. ♎ ♐ ♒
d. ♉ ♋ ♍

e. ♋ ♍ ♏
f. ♍ ♏ ♑
g. ♏ ♑ ♓
h. ♉ ♑ ♓

1. Someone who is a frugal and meticulous homemaker. _____
2. A person who is ambitious and emotionally hard-driving, but also has compassion. _____
3. An individual who initiates in social situations and enjoys being the center of attention. _____
4. Someone whose interest in mysticism is tempered by practicality and conservatism. _____
5. A person who needs a degree of independence but who might share philosophical ideas with a partner. _____
6. One who is highly emotional and wishes to serve and be protective of others. _____
7. Somebody who is artistic and philosophical, but is a little pompous. _____
8. An individual who is an emotionally intense, detail-oriented executive. _____

EXERCISE 17   Sign Combinations 3

The purpose of this group of exercises is to help the student integrate the characteristics of three signs. The descriptions isolate one possible key word for each sign involved, but there are other probable manifestations of the same combination.
Place the most appropriate letter next to each description.

a. ♈ ♐ ♒
b. ♉ ♊ ♋
c. ♈ ♌ ♐
d. ♋ ♎ ♑
e. ♊ ♌ ♎
f. ♌ ♏ ♒
g. ♊ ♍ ♒
h. ♈ ♒ ♓

1. A person who would have a strong sense of duty toward a partner and be protective of the partner as well. _____
2. An individual who is a domineering and emotionally persistent revolutionary. _____
3. Someone who is frugal in the home and enjoys sociability there. _____
4. An individual who is self-assertive in fighting for humanitarian causes because of empathy for the people involved. _____
5. Somebody who serves humanitarian causes by writing about them. _____
6. One who is warm, enthusiastic and zealous. _____
7. A person who would take the initiative in causes for foreign countries. _____
8. Someone who is diplomatic, articulate and warm-hearted. _____

EXERCISE 18 — Sign Combinations 4

The purpose of this group of exercises is to help the student integrate the characteristics of three signs. The descriptions isolate one possible key word for each sign involved, but there are other probable manifestations of the same combination.

Place the most appropriate letter next to each description.

a. ♈ ♉ ♊
b. ♋ ♍ ♓
c. ♍ ♐ ♓
d. ♋ ♌ ♐

e. ♐ ♑ ♒
f. ♉ ♋ ♑
g. ♊ ♍ ♏
h. ♏ ♒ ♓

1. An individual who has a jovial attitude about serving others and being self-sacrificing. _____
2. One who is emotionally intense and self-sacrificing in his protection of others. _____
3. Somebody who is warm, motherly and outgoing. _____
4. An individual who persistently pursues humanitarian causes with deep emotion and compassion. _____
5. A person who voices criticism in an intensely emotional way. _____
6. Someone who has a strong sense of duty, and is possessive in his protection of home and children. _____
7. A person who is articulate, aggressive and persistent. _____
8. One who satisfies his status need by following a career in law and championing humanitarian causes. _____

EXERCISE 19 — Sign Combinations 5

The purpose of this group of exercises is to help the student integrate the characteristics of three signs. The descriptions isolate one possible key word for each sign involved, but there are other probable manifestations of the same combination.

Place the most appropriate letter next to each description.

a. ♊ ♋ ♌
b. ♉ ♍ ♑
c. ♈ ♊ ♋
d. ♈ ♐ ♑

e. ♊ ♍ ♐
f. ♋ ♎ ♓
g. ♉ ♌ ♏
h. ♋ ♌ ♍

1. Somebody who is ambitious and energetically pursues a career in law. _____
2. One who initiates and is sociable in the home. _____
3. A person who enjoys sharing and even sacrificing himself for a partner in the home. _____
4. An individual who is critical and domineering in the home. _____
5. Someone who is a motherly, communicative actor. _____
6. An individual who is practical, pays attention to detail and is persistent and ambitious. _____
7. A person who is stubborn or persistent and may be domineering and emotional. _____
8. Someone who is articulate but may be critical and tactless. _____

19

EXERCISE 20　　　　　　　　Sign Combinations 6

The purpose of this group of exercises is to help the student integrate the characteristics of three signs. The descriptions isolate one possible key word for each sign involved, but there are other probable manifestations of the same combination.

Place the most appropriate letter next to each description.

a. ♈ ♋ ♎
b. ♑ ♒ ♓
c. ♊ ♍ ♓
d. ♎ ♏ ♐
e. ♌ ♍ ♓
f. ♈ ♉ ♋
g. ♋ ♌ ♑
h. ♎ ♐ ♒

1. A person who is an energetic but practical mother. _____

2. An individual who is an empathetic actor but also pays close attention to detail. _____

3. Someone who is a fair-minded humanitarian and therefore is excellent in foreign diplomatic affairs. _____

4. An individual who is interested in humanitarian causes and has both a strong sense of duty and compassion. _____

5. A person whose strong sense of duty is dramatically exhibited in the home. _____

6. One who probes the mind intensely to find a philosophy which helps give him peace and harmony. _____

7. Somebody who is extremely adaptable and gregarious, compassionate and service-oriented. _____

8. Someone who may be aggressive with the partner in the home. _____

EXERCISE 21　　　　　　　　Sign Combinations 7

The purpose of this group of exercises is to help the student integrate the characteristics of three signs. The descriptions isolate one possible key word for each sign involved, but there are other probable manifestations of the same combination.

Place the most appropriate letter next to each description.

a. ♍ ♎ ♏
b. ♊ ♐ ♓
c. ♋ ♐ ♒
d. ♈ ♌ ♑

e. ♏ ♐ ♑
f. ♊ ♎ ♒
g. ♉ ♌ ♒
h. ♉ ♍ ♎

1. An individual who is loyal and helpful to a partner but is critical and possessive as well. _____
2. Someone who is an emotionally hard-driving and ambitious athlete. _____
3. A person who is compassionate, sociable and philosophical. _____
4. One whose need for freedom would be tempered by practicality and the desire to be the center of attention. _____
5. An individual who might like freedom and distant travel, as long as he has a home base to which to return. _____
6. A person whose artistic ability is directed toward detailed work in crafts. _____
7. Somebody who is gregarious and articulate on a one-to-one basis and in groups. _____
8. An individual who is an ambitious actor with tremendous zeal and aggressiveness. _____

EXERCISE 22 Sign Combinations 8

The purpose of this group of exercises is to help the student integrate the characteristics of the three signs. The descriptions isolate one possible key word for each sign involved, but there are other probable manifestations of the same combination.

Place the most appropriate letter next to each description.

a. ♊ ♌ ♐
b. ♋ ♍ ♑
c. ♎ ♏ ♒
d. ♈ ♊ ♓

e. ♈ ♎ ♑
f. ♉ ♊ ♓
g. ♍ ♏ ♐
h. ♋ ♌ ♒

1. Someone whose strong sense of duty and desire to be service-oriented are directed toward protection of the home. _____

2. An individual who might be possessive of the partner but who also needs a degree of independence. _____

3. One who is outspoken, sociable and enjoys being the center of attention. _____

4. A person who does deeply probing work (physical or mental) in foreign countries. _____

5. Somebody who is articulate and gregarious, has an emotional need to help people and has the persistence and practicality to accomplish his goal. _____

6. An individual who is aggressively ambitious in a charming way. _____

7. One who is warm-hearted and motherly toward peers. _____

8. Somebody who is aggressive and articulate in helping to rescue other individuals. _____

EXERCISE 23   Sign Combinations 9

The purpose of this group of exercises is to help the student integrate the characteristics of three signs. The descriptions isolate one possible key word for each sign involved, but there are other probable manifestations of the same combination.

Place the most appropriate letter next to each description.

a. ♉ ♍ ♒
b. ♋ ♌ ♎
c. ♌ ♍ ♑
d. ♎ ♍ ♓

e. ♊ ♋ ♍
f. ♍ ♎ ♒
g. ♈ ♎ ♐
h. ♊ ♒ ♓

1. An individual who enjoys serving a partner or groups of peers. _____
2. Someone who writes about humanitarian matters with compassion and empathy. _____
3. A person whose compassion and emotional intensity are directed toward obtaining justice. _____
4. One who is possessive in the home but enjoys socializing there as well. _____
5. An individual who is critical, ambitious and domineering. _____
6. Somebody who might initiate and travel to distant places with a partner. _____
7. A person who pursues humanitarian idealism with practical persistence and emotional intensity. _____
8. One who is protective toward his partner and generous with him. _____

EXERCISE 24   Sign Combinations 10

The purpose of this group of exercises is to help the student integrate the characteristics of three signs. The descriptions isolate one possible key word for each sign involved, but there are other probable manifestations of the same combination.

Place the most appropriate letter next to each description.
a. ♊ ♋ ♓
b. ♌ ♏ ♓
c. ♋ ♏ ♑
d. ♉ ♊ ♎

e. ♉ ♍ ♒
f. ♈ ♐ ♓
g. ♐ ♑ ♓
h. ♈ ♉ ♏

1. Someone who works toward humanitarian goals in a practical and persistent way, with all details considered. _____

2. A person who is a hard-driving executive with an emotional, even motherly attitude toward his employees. _____

3. One who zealously initiates in the areas of religion and mysticism. _____

4. An individual whose sociability emerges in mothering and in sacrificing himself for others. _____

5. Somebody whose initiative is directed toward material goals with emotional intensity. _____

6. A person who has dramatic ability, can empathize with his roles and has the emotional persistence to pursue a career in acting. _____

7. One who has artistic ability in a craft that involves great dexterity. _____

8. An individual whose strong sense of duty is combined with religious feelings and compassion for others. _____

EXERCISE 25   Sign Combinations 11

The purpose of this group of exercises is to help the student integrate the characteristics of three signs. The descriptions isolate one possible key word for each sign involved, but there are other probable manifestations of the same combination.

Place the most appropriate letter next to each description.

a. ♎ ♐ ♓
b. ♉ ♋ ♎
c. ♍ ♏ ♒
d. ♊ ♐ ♒

e. ♈ ♏ ♐
f. ♌ ♎ ♏
g. ♉ ♏ ♑
h. ♊ ♍ ♑

1. A person who is sociable and has a strong sense of duty about serving others. _____
2. An individual who is analytical and searches deeply while working on humanitarian ideals. _____
3. Someone who is persistent or stubborn and could direct his hard-driving aggressiveness toward raising his status and acquiring material possessions. _____
4. Somebody who enjoys communicating his philosophical ideas to groups of like-minded persons. _____
5. One who is domineering and possessive in partnership. _____
6. An individual who has strong loyalty to a partner and is frugal in the home. _____
7. Someone who displays empathy and philosophical understanding of the partner. _____
8. A person who is an intensely emotional and zealous clergyman, but who may think of himself first. _____

EXERCISE 26　　　　　　　Sign Combinations 12

The purpose of this group of exercises is to help the student integrate the characteristics of three signs. The descriptions isolate one possible key word for each sign involved, but there are other probable manifestations of same combination.

Place the most appropriate letter next to each description.

a. ♈ ♒ ♓　　　　e. ♋ ♌ ♓
b. ♉ ♋ ♍　　　　f. ♎ ♑ ♒
c. ♋ ♎ ♒　　　　g. ♊ ♍ ♑
d. ♍ ♐ ♑　　　　h. ♈ ♉ ♑

1. One who has empathy and will aggressively pursue humanitarian causes. _____
2. An individual who combines his ambition and emotionally hard-driving ability in his writing. _____
3. Somebody who is practical and possessive in the home. _____
4. A person who is warm-hearted and self-sacrificing in the protection of others. _____
5. An individual who is aggressive in situations that involve status and material rewards. _____
6. Someone who needs a home and partner but must retain a degree of independence as well. _____
7. A person who can discipline his tendency to be critical and tactless. _____
8. One whose sense of duty is directed toward both partner and groups of peers. _____

EXERCISE 27   Houses

Houses in the horoscope represent areas of the life. Place the appropriate number next to each house description given below.

1. First House
2. Second House
3. Third House
4. Fourth House
5. Fifth House
6. Sixth House
7. Seventh House
8. Eighth House
9. Ninth House
10. Tenth House
11. Eleventh House
12. Twelfth House

a. Career, profession, relations with the outer world, social status; house of the more distantly-linked parent. _____

b. Partnerships, including marriage; close friendships, contracts, the public, open enemies. _____

c. The personality, physical appearance and physical make-up, beginnings, childhood; the house of the "I." _____

d. Concealment, mysticism, occultism, self-undoing, subconscious, limitations, mental health, confinement (in prisons, hospitals, etc.), institutions, large animals. _____

e. One's own possessions, finances, and other material resources; earning capacity, utilization of material objects, deep values, feelings of self- worth. _____

f. Physical health, service, subordinates, routine, daily work, small animals. _____

g. Large groups and organizations, impersonal relationships, acquaintances, peers, hopes and wishes. _____

h. Direct and immediate relations and communication, brothers and sisters, neighbors, letters, telephones, newspapers, short journeys. _____

i. Philosophy, religion, law, world-view, long journeys, higher education, sports, publishing, in-laws. _____

j. Home, ancestry, origins, foundation, where one feels securely at home, endings, old age; house of the more closely-linked parent. _____

k. Creative self-expression; offspring, literal and figurative; love affairs, artistic creativity, entertainment, speculation. _____

l. Other peoples' possessions and finances, inheritance, banking, taxes, death, sex, regeneration. _____

EXERCISE 28

Signs in Houses 1

All twelve signs of the zodiac are part of each horoscope. The way each sign is expressed is dependent upon the planets in the sign and the houses which contain the sign.

The sign or signs in each house indicate the general requirements of that house. The purpose of the following exercises is to integrate the definitions of the houses with the characteristics of the signs. Each phrase corresponds to a particular sign in a particular house. The key words given are only samples of the possibilities. Also, in actual charts a house usually contains more than one sign. Therefore, when interpreting a chart always blend the characteristics of all the signs in a given house. [E.g., Capricorn and Aquarius in the first house means that freedom and independence (Aquarius), as well as seriousness and responsibility (Capricorn), are important in the general personality (first house).]

Place the most appropriate letter next to each phrase given below.

a. ♈ in the seventh house
b. ♉ in the second house
c. ♊ in the eleventh house
d. ♋ in the ninth house
e. ♌ in the sixth house
f. ♍ in the third house
g. ♎ in the fourth house
h. ♏ in the twelfth house
i. ♐ in the eighth house
j. ♑ in the tenth house
k. ♒ in the fifth house
l. ♓ in the first house

1. Confused about self, or the personality has an aura of spirituality. _____
2. Wants his children to be independent. _____
3. Ambitious and status-oriented in career. _____
4. Enjoys peace, harmony and beauty in the home. _____
5. Careful about expenditures with his own finances—wants to get his money's worth. _____
6. Analyzes or is critical in writing and speaking. _____
7. Gregarious with groups of peers. _____
8. Either takes the initiative in partnership or gives the initiative to the partner. _____
9. Philosophical about the life and death cycle. _____
10. Intensely emotional about mysticism and the occult. _____
11. May make one's home in a foreign country. _____
12. Likes to be the center of attention at work. _____

EXERCISE 29 — Signs in Houses 2

The sign or signs in each house indicate the general requirements of that house. Place the most appropriate letter next to each phrase given below.

a. ♈ in the fourth house
b. ♉ in the eighth house
c. ♊ in the twelfth house
d. ♋ in the eleventh house
e. ♌ in the second house
f. ♍ in the ninth house
g. ♎ in the sixth house
h. ♏ in the fifth house
i. ♐ in the third house
j. ♑ in the first house
k. ♒ in the seventh house
l. ♓ in the tenth house

1. Self-sacrificing in career. _____
2. Energetic or initiating in the home. _____
3. Careful and practical about expenditure of other people's resources. _____
4. Generous with one's own resources. _____
5. Enjoys communicating about the mystical and occult. _____
6. Needs independence in partnerships or is attracted to unusual partners. _____
7. Has a serious, conservative personality. _____
8. Feels at home with groups of peers and may even mother them. _____
9. Wants harmony and peace in the daily work situation. _____
10. Communicates enthusiastically and sometimes tactlessly with brothers and sisters. _____
11. Has deep emotional involvement with one's children and may be possessive of them. _____
12 Has a detailed and analytical philosophy of life. _____

EXERCISE 30 — Signs in Houses 3

The sign or signs in each house indicate the general requirements of that house. Place the most appropriate letter next to each phrase given below.

a. ♈ in the fifth house
b. ♉ in the ninth house
c. ♊ in the third house
d. ♋ in the first house
e. ♌ in the seventh house
f. ♍ in the tenth house
g. ♎ in the second house
h. ♏ in the sixth house
i. ♐ in the twelfth house
j. ♑ in the fourth house
k. ♒ in the eleventh house
l. ♓ in the eighth house

1. Emotional and self-sacrificing in sexual matters. ____
2. Detail-oriented in career and can be involved in a service-oriented occupation. ____
3. Initiating or aggressive in love affairs. ____
4. Involved with humanitarian groups or needs independence in group activities. ____
5. Earns one's living through the fine arts. ____
6. Involved in an organized religion which provides material security. ____
7. Philosophically involved with the mystical and occult. ____
8. Communications with siblings are important. ____
9. Enjoys a partner who is warm and outgoing, or attracted to a partner who will allow the individual to be the center of attention. ____
10. Disciplined or conservative in the home. ____
11. Emotionally hard-driving and deep-probing in daily work. ____
12. Has a motherly and protective personality. ____

EXERCISE 31   Signs in Houses 4

The sign or signs in each house indicate the general requirements of that house. Place the most appropriate letter next to each phrase given below.

a. ♈ in the third house
b. ♉ in the sixth house
c. ♊ in the first house
d. ♋ in the seventh house
e. ♌ in the eleventh house
f. ♍ in the eighth house
g. ♎ in the fifth house
h. ♏ in the fourth house
i. ♐ in the tenth house
j. ♑ in the twelfth house
k. ♒ in the second house
l. ♓ in the ninth house

1. Enjoys performing before large groups. _____
2. Communicates energetically, or takes the initiative in relations with siblings. _____
3. Spiritual needs are satisfied through religion. _____
4. Career may involve distant travel. _____
5. May be possessive and emotional in the home. _____
6. Unchanging routine important in daily work. _____
7. Handles other people's resources practically and with great detail. _____
8. Practical and persistent in investigating the occult. _____
9. Sociability is important to the individual. _____
10. Treats one's children as partners. _____
11. Motherly and protective of the partner. _____
12. Earns one's living through modern technology. _____

EXERCISE 32

Signs in Houses 5

The sign or signs in each house indicate the general requirements of that house. Place the most appropriate letter next to each phrase given below.

a. ♈ in the second house
b. ♉ in the tenth house
c. ♊ in the seventh house
d. ♋ in the sixth house
e. ♌ in the twelfth house
f. ♍ in the fourth house
g. ♎ in the eighth house
h. ♏ in the ninth house
i. ♐ in the fifth house
j. ♑ in the third house
k. ♒ in the first house
l. ♓ in the eleventh house

1. Is an individualist and needs personal freedom. _____
2. Energetic and initiating in order to earn one's living. _____
3. Might be domineering in relations with institutions. _____
4. Serious and disciplined in communication. _____
5. May have a career in an artistic craft. _____
6. Regeneration might occur through a partner. _____
7. Takes long journeys with one's children. _____
8. Motherly and protective in the daily work situation. _____
9. Probes deeply into philosophy. _____
10. Compassion and emotional involvement with peers. _____
11. Needs a partner who is gregarious and communicative. _____
12. Meticulous and fussy in the home. _____

EXERCISE 33   **Signs in Houses 6**

The sign or signs in each house indicate the general requirements of that house. Place the most appropriate letter next to each phrase given below.

a. ♈ in the eighth house
b. ♉ in the fourth house
c. ♊ in the second house
d. ♋ in the fifth house
e. ♌ in the third house
f. ♍ in the eleventh house
g. ♎ in the tenth house
h. ♏ in the first house
i. ♐ in the seventh house
j. ♑ in the ninth house
k. ♒ in the twelfth house
l. ♓ in the sixth house

1. Service-oriented in humanitarian causes. _____
2. Frugal and practical in the home. _____
3. Empathetic and emotionally involved with co-workers. _____
4. Initiating and possibly aggressive in the area of sexuality. _____
5. Communicates dramatically. _____
6. Might have a foreign partner. _____
7. An emotionally intense and secretive personality. _____
8. Career as a mediator or in the fine arts. _____
9. Strongly protective of one's children. _____
10. Has original ideas about the mystical and occult. _____
11. Earns one's living through verbal or written communications. _____
12. Higher education may be delayed, or the individual is disciplined in pursuits of the higher mind. _____

EXERCISE 34   Signs in Houses 7

The sign or sign in each house indicate the general requirements of that house. Place the most appropriate letter next to each phrase given below.

a. ♈ in the eleventh house
b. ♉ in the first house
c. ♊ in the fourth house
d. ♋ in the eighth house
e. ♌ in the tenth house
f. ♍ in the fifth house
g. ♎ in the third house
h. ♏ in the seventh house
i. ♐ in the second house
j. ♑ in the sixth house
k. ♒ in the ninth house
l. ♓ in the twelfth house

1. Self-sacrificing in institutions, such as hospitals and prisons. _____
2. Initiating and aggressive with peers. _____
3. May have a career in acting. _____
4. May earn one's living in a foreign country, _____
5. Practicality and persistence are important attributes of the personality. _____
6. Wishes harmony with brothers and sisters. _____
7. Disciplined or inhibited in the daily work situation. _____
8. Protective of other people's money. _____
9. Emotional intensity and possessiveness in the partnership area. _____
10. Ideas on religion are original and individualistic. _____
11. Sociability is important in the home area. _____
12. May be critical of one's children. _____

EXERCISE 35   **Signs in Houses 8**

The sign or signs in each house indicate the general requirements of that house. Place the most appropriate letter next to each phrase given below.

a. ♈ in the first house
b. ♉ in the third house
c. ♊ in the ninth house
d. ♋ in the twelfth house
e. ♌ in the fourth house
f. ♍ in the second house
g. ♎ in the seventh house
h. ♏ in the eleventh house
i. ♐ in the sixth house
j. ♑ in the eighth house
k. ♒ in the tenth house
l. ♓ in the fifth house

1. Earn one's living as a critic. _____
2. Enjoys being the center of attention in the home. _____
3. Has an energetic and initiating personality. _____
4. Self-sacrificing toward one's children. _____
5. Emotionally intense toward peers, and possessive of them. _____
6. Is sociable in foreign countries. _____
7. Is motherly and protective in institutions. _____
8. A career in modern technology or needs independence in career. _____
9. Is jovial in the daily work situation. _____
10. Needs a harmonious partnership. _____
11. Conservative with other people's resources. _____
12. Is practical with siblings and possessive of them. _____

EXERCISE 36

Signs in Houses 9

The sign or signs in each house indicate the general requirements of that house. Place the most appropriate letter next to each phrase given below.

a. ♈ in the sixth house
b. ♉ in the fifth house
c. ♊ in the sixth house
d. ♋ in the fourth house
e. ♌ in the fifth house
f. ♍ in the first house
g. ♎ in the first house
h. ♏ in the third house
i. ♐ in the fourth house
j. ♑ in the second house
k. ♒ in the third house
l. ♓ in the second house

1. Warm, enthusiastic and generous with one's children. _____
2. Is ambitious in earning one's living. _____
3. Communicates in an unusual way. _____
4. May make one's home in a foreign country. _____
5. Aggressive and initiating at work. _____
6. Possessive of, and has emotional, intense feelings toward siblings. _____
7. May earn one's living through sacrificing for others. _____
8. Charming personality. _____
9. Practical but stubborn in dealing with one's children. _____
10. Adaptable and sociable at work. _____
11. Needs protection and emotional security at home. _____
12. Is meticulous about one's personal appearance. _____

EXERCISE 37   **Signs in Houses 10**

The sign or signs in each house indicate the general requirements of that house. Place the most appropriate letter next to each phrase given below.

a. ♈ in the twelfth house
b. ♉ in the seventh house
c. ♊ in the eighth house
d. ♋ in the tenth house
e. ♌ in the ninth house
f. ♍ in the twelfth house
g. ♎ in the eleventh house
h. ♏ in the tenth house
i. ♐ in the ninth house
j. ♑ in the eleventh house
k. ♒ in the eighth house
l. ♓ in the seventh house

1. Service-oriented in institutions. _____
2. Is practical about partnerships and looks to the partner for material security. _____
3. Has unusual ideas about sex. _____
4. Is motherly in career or works from the home. _____
5. Has a philosophical approach to religion. _____
6. Is charming in groups or is a good group mediator. _____
7. Has a career in which his deep-probing quality is utilized. _____
8. Self-sacrificing for a partner. _____
9. Pursues the study of dramatics in higher education. _____
10. Joins serious groups or feels responsible for one's peers. _____
11. Self-assertive when dealing with the mystical and occult. _____
12. Articulate on the subjects of sex, death and regeneration. _____

EXERCISE 38   Planets

Planets represent functions or energies. The signs in which the planets are posited show *how* these energies are expressed; the houses which contain the planets indicate *where* the energies are directly manifested; and the aspects denote whether or not these energies are easily utilized.

Place the appropriate letter next to the key words for each planet given below.

a. ☉   f. ♃
b. ☽   g. ♄
c. ☿   h. ♅
d. ♀   i. ♆
e. ♂   j. ♇

1. Response, emotion, intuition, fluctuation; the maternal function. _____
2. Love, affection, pleasure, artistry, harmonization, indolence; female sexuality. _____
3. Total transformation through elimination and renewal, violence, subterranean (subconscious) eruption, unrelenting power; deep-probing analysis. _____
4. Vitalization, the directly expressed self, exercise of ego-identity and will; the paternal function. _____
5. Refined sensitivity, spirituality, dissolution, confusion, deception, illusion, intoxication; ethereal and spiritual artistry. _____
6. Wide-ranging and complex thinking, wisdom, which are functions of the "higher mind"; joy, optimism, success, excess; expansion. _____
7. Deviation, liberation, sudden or revolutionary change; technique and technology. _____
8. Verbal skills, communication, perception, logical thinking, cleverness, wit, which are functions of the "lower mind". _____
9. Contraction, containment, crystallization, responsibility, structure, discipline, channeling, limitation, restriction, frustration, gloom, pessimism; punishment. _____
10. Initiative, aggressive action, courage, violence, passion; male sexuality. _____

EXERCISE 39　　　　　　　　Planets in Houses 1

The first group of exercises involving the planets combine them with houses. There are meanings other than those given for these combinations.

Place the appropriate letter next to each description given below.

a. ☉ in the ninth house
b. ☽ in the first house
c. ☿ in the fifth house
d. ♀ in the third house
e. ♂ in the fourth house
f. ♃ in the sixth house
g. ♄ in the second house
h. ♅ in the eleventh house
i. ♆ in the seventh house
j. ♇ in the tenth house

1. Has a moody personality or is an emotionally sensitive person. _____
2. Is energetic and initiates in the home or is argumentative in the home. _____
3. Watches carefully over one's own finances, or earning capacity is limited. _____
4. Wants power in career or makes a forceful executive. _____
5. Communicates artistically or lazy about writing letters. _____
6. Idealizes the partner or is confused by the partner. _____
7. Enjoys his daily work or overextends himself at work. _____
8. Communications with his children are important or talks excessively with a lover. _____
9. Satisfies his ego needs through his religion or is able to throw himself whole-heartedly into foreign affairs. _____
10. Joins unusual groups or is too independent to join groups. _____

EXERCISE 40 — Planets in Houses 2

Place the appropriate letter next to each description given below.

a. ☉ in the fourth house
b. ☽ in the tenth house
c. ☿ in the twelfth house
d. ♀ in the fifth house
e. ♂ in the sixth house
f. ♃ in the eleventh house
g. ♄ in the eighth house
h. ♅ in the seventh house
i. ♆ in the first house
j. ♇ in the third house

1. Has sexual problems or watches over other people's money carefully. _____
2. Needs independence in partnerships, or has unusual partners. _____
3. Works with the public through the career, or mother influenced career. _____
4. Communicates powerfully or monopolizes conversations. _____
5. Confused about oneself or is a spiritual person. _____
6. Overextends oneself in group activities or develops through peers. _____
7. Industrious in the daily work situation or may be too aggressive at work. _____
8. Artistically creative or over-indulges one's children. _____
9. Enjoys discussing the mystical, or verbal communications may be difficult. _____
10. Ego satisfaction through the home or may consider one's own ego first in mothering. _____

EXERCISE 41 Planets in Houses 3

Place the appropriate letter next to each description given below.

a. ☉ in the fifth house
b. ☽ in the second house
c. ☿ in the tenth house
d. ♀ in the eleventh house
e. ♂ in the first house

f. ♃ in the eighth house
g. ♄ in the sixth house
h. ♅ in the third house
i. ♆ in the fourth house
j. ♇ in the seventh house

1. Has an energetic or aggressive personality. _____
2. Wishes to control one's partner or is deeply analytical about one-to- one relationships. _____
3. Receives ego gratification through one's children, or creativity is important to development of the ego. _____
4. Confused home, or home is a sanctuary. _____
5. Fluctuating about self-worth or earns one's living by dealing with the public. _____
6. Is restricted in daily work, or ordered routine is essential in the work situation. _____
7. Communications are important in career, or does a great deal of public speaking. _____
8. Takes sudden short trips, or is erratic in communications. _____
9. Inherits a great deal of money, or over-indulges in sex. _____
10. Enjoys group activities, or is lazy in working toward fulfillment of hopes and wishes. _____

EXERCISE 42   Planets in Houses 4

Place the appropriate letter next to each description given below.
- a. ☉ in the first house
- b. ☽ in the third house
- c. ☿ in the first house
- d. ♀ in the second house
- e. ♂ in the third house
- f. ♃ in the fifth house
- g. ♄ in the fourth house
- h. ♅ in the fifth house
- i. ♆ in the sixth house
- j. ♇ in the sixth house

1. Earns one's living through art, or enjoys spending one's own money. _____
2. Wants to be boss in the daily work situation, or deep-probing analysis is part of the daily routine. _____
3. Vital energy is strong in the personality, or ego gratification is an important element in the personality. _____
4. Feels responsibility in the home, or home situation is limiting. _____
5. Is confused at work, or is self-sacrificing with co-workers. _____
6. Communicates emotionally, or is motherly toward brothers and sisters. _____
7. Has unusual children, or needs independence in love affairs. _____
8. Active communications are essential to the personality, or cleverness and wit are expressed through the personality. _____
9. Communicates aggressively, or is the neighborhood initiator. _____
10. Has had many love affairs, or receives tremendous pleasure from one's children. _____

EXERCISE 43

Planets in Houses 5

Place the appropriate letter next to each description given below.

a. ☉ in the seventh house
b. ☽ in the eleventh house
c. ☿ in the seventh house
d. ♀ in the tenth house
e. ♂ in the eighth house
f. ♃ in the twelfth house
g. ♄ in the ninth house
h. ♅ in the twelfth house
i. ♆ in the eighth house
j. ♇ in the eleventh house

1. Speaks foreign languages, or likes to write about philosophy and religion. _____
2. Powerful and controlling in large groups, or is deep-probing and analytical when peers are involved. _____
3. Has unusual ideas about the mystical and occult, or is an institutional reformer. _____
4. Throws oneself whole-heartedly into partnership, or receives ego gratification through partners. _____
5. Belongs to an organized religion, or distant travel is limited. _____
6. Enjoys studying the subconscious and unconscious mind, or the mystical and occult are important to one's philosophy. _____
7. Has a career in art, or makes a charming impression on the world. _____
8. May not handle other people's money competently, or has spiritual feelings about sex. _____
9. Is sentimental about humanitarian causes, or is motherly toward peers. _____
10. May be sexually aggressive, or energetically uses other people's resources. _____

EXERCISE 44　　　　　　　　　　Planets in Houses 6

Place the appropriate letter next to each description given below.

a. ☉ in the third house 　　f. ♃ in the first house
b. ☽ in the fifth house 　　 g. ♄ in the fifth house
c. ☿ in the third house 　　h. ♅ in the first house
d. ♀ in the first house 　　 i. ♆ in the third house
e. ♂ in the fifth house 　　 j. ♇ in the first house

1. Feels heavy responsibility about one's children or serious about love affairs. _____
2. Forceful personality or deeply analytical about self. _____
3. Articulate with brothers and sisters or talkative on short trips. _____
4. Charming personality or self-indulgent. _____
5. Gets lost easily on short trips or communicates imaginatively. _____
6. Ego needs are gratified through siblings or throws oneself into neighborhood affairs. _____
7. Unusual person, or independence is an important attribute of the personality. _____
8. Jovial personality, or may be overweight. _____
9. Aggressive in love affairs, or takes the initiative with one's children. _____
10. Is very motherly toward one's children, or experiences fluctuations in love affairs. _____

EXERCISE 45   Planets in Houses 7

Place the appropriate letter next to each description given below.
- a. ☉ in the eleventh house
- b. ☽ in the seventh house
- c. ☿ in the eleventh house
- d. ♀ in the ninth house
- e. ♂ in the eleventh house
- f. ♃ in the seventh house
- g. ♄ in the seventh house
- h. ♅ in the ninth house
- i. ♆ in the eleventh house
- j. ♇ in the ninth house

1. Aggressive with peers or takes the initiative in organizations. _____
2. Concerned about power in foreign affairs or deeply analytical about religion. _____
3. Needs a partner who helps the individual to grow and develop or may marry more than once. _____
4. Receives ego satisfaction through organizations or "shines" when with peers. _____
5. Takes pleasure in distant travel or appreciates the beauty of foreign languages. _____
6. Mothers the partner or has emotional fluctuation in partnerships. _____
7. Enjoys speaking before groups or is articulate about humanitarian causes. _____
8. Does not conform to organized religions or takes unexpected long journeys. _____
9. Belongs to spiritual groups or is confused in large groups. _____
10. Strong sense of responsibility toward the partner or marries late. _____

EXERCISE 46   Planets in Houses 8

Place the appropriate letter next to each description given below.
a. ☉ in the sixth house   f. ♃ in the fourth house
b. ☽ in the fourth house   g. ♄ in the tenth house
c. ☿ in the second house   h. ♅ in the eighth house
d. ♀ in the sixth house   i. ♆ in the twelfth house
e. ♂ in the second house   j. ♇ in the eighth house

1. Grows and develops in the home or enjoys philosophical discussions in or about the home. _____
2. Cultivates spirituality through mysticism and the occult or does not have a clear understanding of the subconscious mind. _____
3. Serious and disciplined in career, or limitations in career. _____
4. Motherly in the home or deep emotional attachment to the home. _____
5. Charming at work or lazy in the daily work situation. _____
6. Deeply analytical about sex, death and regeneration or obtains power through other people's resources. _____
7. Energetically expresses one's values or aggressive in acquiring material possessions. _____
8. Throws oneself whole-heartedly into daily work situation or receives ego gratfication through the daily routine. _____
9. Earns one's living through communications or enjoys communicating about one's values. _____
10. Unusual ideas about sex or erratic in the use of other people's resources. _____

EXERCISE 47   Planets, Signs, Houses 1

The purpose of this group of exercises is to integrate planets with houses and signs. The houses, of course, represent areas; the signs in houses denote general requirements of those given areas; the planets in houses describe more specific needs in these particular areas. The statements do not include all possibilities.

Place the most appropriate letter next to each statement given below.

a. ☉ in ♍ in the eleventh house
b. ☽ in ♎ in the sixth house
c. ☿ in ♌ in the tenth house
d. ♀ in ♑ in the fourth house
e. ♂ in ♈ in the seventh house
f. ♃ in ♊ in the second house
g. ♄ in ♓ in the first house
h. ♅ in ♉ in the ninth house
i. ♆ in ♍ in the third house
j. ♇ in ♋ in the eighth house

1. Needs an established religion for a sense of material security but uses originality in interpreting the doctrines. _____

2. Chooses an aggressive partner whom he allows to take the initiative in the relationship or is the aggressive and initiating partner. _____
3. Needs security and status in the home and wants to be surrounded by beauty there, although this beauty may be conservative and austere. _____
4. Self-sacrifice and a strong sense of responsibility are important attributes of the personality. _____
5. Is protective and yet enjoys the power gained from handling other people's resources. _____
6. Likes to have detailed directions for short trips but may get lost anyway. _____
7. Likes to be the center of attention in his career and obtains this attention through communications. _____
8. Has intense emotional involvement with groups and obtains ego satisfaction through these groups. _____
9. Works best in the daily routine with another individual with whom there may be an emotional involvement or whom the native mothers. _____
10. May earn one's living through communication which must provide growth for the individual or great remunerative rewards. _____

47

EXERCISE 48　　　　　　　　Planets, Signs, Houses 2

Place the most appropriate letter next to each statement given below.

a. ☉ in ♒ in the twelfth house　　f. ♃ in ♊ in the sixth house
b. ☽ in ♓ in the eleventh house　g. ♄ in ♋ in the eighth house
c. ☿ in ♈ in the third house　　　h. ♅ in ♌ in the first house
d. ♀ in ♉ in the second house　　i. ♆ in ♎ in the seventh house
e. ♂ in ♍ in the fifth house　　　j. ♇ in ♌ in the ninth house

1. Grows and develops through socializing in daily work. _____

2. Gains ego gratification from unusual occult activities. _____

3. Needs a partner with whom to share and may idealize the partner. _____

4. Communicates energetically, especially with brothers and sisters. _____

5. May have power and be the center of attention in foreign countries. _____

6. Has an unusual and dramatic personality. _____

7. Is disciplined and protective in handling other people's resources. _____

8. May be aggressive with, and critical of, one's children. _____

9. May earn one's living from arts and crafts. _____

10. Motherly and self-sacrificing with peers. _____

EXERCISE 49   Planets, Signs, Houses 3

Place the most appropriate letter next to each statement given below.

a. ☉ in ♈ in the fourth house
b. ☽ in ♍ in the twelfth house
c. ☿ in ♐ in the fifth house
d. ♀ in ♒ in the eighth house
e. ♂ in ♉ in the third house
f. ♃ in ♓ in the eleventh house
g. ♄ in ♍ in the sixth house
h. ♅ in ♋ in the seventh house
i. ♆ in ♌ in the first house
j. ♇ in ♎ in the second house

1. Earns one's living through wielding power in the art world. _____

2. Discusses philosophy with one's children. _____

3. Is disciplined and detail-oriented at work. _____

4. Receives ego satisfaction through initiating in the home. _____

5. Develops and grows by sacrificing for humanitarian causes. _____

6. Has a dramatic and charismatic personality. _____

7. Is highly intuitive and probes with deep emotionality into the occult and mystical. _____

8. Enjoys sexual activity but wishes also to remain independent in that area. _____

9. Initiates and is persistent with brothers and sisters. _____

10. Has an unusual partner whom the native mothers and protects. _____

EXERCISE 50 Planets, Signs, Houses 4

Place the most appropriate letter next to each statement given below.

a. ☉ in ♋ in the first house
b. ☽ in ♒ in the fifth house
c. ☿ in ♎ in the eleventh house
d. ♀ in ♐ in the ninth house
e. ♂ in ♓ in the eighth house
f. ♃ in ♉ in the seventh house
g. ♄ in ♏ in the third house
h. ♅ in ♈ in the fourth house
i. ♆ in ♊ in the tenth house
j. ♇ in ♍ in the twelfth house

1. Aggressive and yet self-sacrificing in the area of sexuality. _____

2. Enjoys distant travel and may deal in art in foreign countries. _____

3. Very powerful and service-oriented in institutions. _____

4. Vitality and motherliness are both attributes of the personality. _____

5. Motherly in an unusual way toward one's children. _____

6. Converses in a serious and emotionally intense manner. _____

7. Is sociable and imaginative in the career. _____

8. Communicates charmingly and artfully before groups. _____

9. Needs a partner who is both philosophical and practical. _____

10. Is energetic and independent at home. _____

EXERCISE 51   Planets, Signs, Houses 5

Place the most appropriate letter next to each statement given below.

a. ☉ in ♊ in the fifth house
b. ☽ in ♈ in the first house
c. ☿ in ♐ in the twelfth house
d. ♀ in ♓ in the tenth house
e. ♂ in ♌ in the sixth house
f. ♃ in ♍ in the eighth house
g. ♄ in ♒ in the seventh house
h. ♅ in ♉ in the fourth house
i. ♆ in ♋ in the second house
j. ♇ in ♏ in the eleventh house

1. Receives pleasure from practicing a helping and healing profession. _____
2. Is emotionally intense and powerful in groups. _____
3. Receives ego gratification from socializing with one's children. _____
4. Earns one's living through self-sacrifice and protection of others. _____
5. Needs independence in partnerships and yet feels responsibility for the partner. _____
6. Outgoing, initiating and domineering at work. _____
7. Has an emotional and aggressive personality. _____
8. Acquires unusual possessions for the home. _____
9. Communicates philosophically about the mystical and occult. _____
10. Works successfully with the details of other people's finances. _____

EXERCISE 52　　　　　　　　Planets, Signs, Houses 6

Place the most appropriate letter next to each statement given below.

a. ☉ in ♍ in the seventh house
b. ☽ in ♌ in the tenth house
c. ☿ in ♏ in the second house
d. ♀ in ♈ in the first house
e. ♂ in ♑ in the ninth house
f. ♃ in ♋ in the third house
g. ♄ in ♐ in the fifth house
h. ♅ in ♊ in the sixth house
i. ♆ in ♏ in the twelfth house
j. ♇ in ♋ in the fourth house

1. Is jovial, motherly and protective toward brothers and sisters. _____

2. Has initiative and discipline in the area of higher education. _____

3. Receives ego satisfaction through the partner but may be critical of the partner as well. _____

4. Sociable but independent at work. _____

5. Being before the public as the center of attention is a requirement of the career. _____

6. Wields power but is also motherly at home. _____

7. Has a charming, outgoing and forceful personality. _____

8. Feels a strong sense of responsibility for one's children and wishes to help them grow and develop philosophically. _____

9. Has intensely emotional and spiritual involvement with the occult. _____

10. Earns one's living through deep-probing consultation. _____

EXERCISE 53　　　　　　　Planets, Signs, Houses 7

Place the most appropriate letter next to each statement given below.

a. ☉ in ♑ in the tenth house
b. ☽ in ♉ in the third house
c. ☿ in ♋ in the first house
d. ♀ in ♌ in the seventh house
e. ♂ in ♊ in the eleventh house
f. ♃ in ♎ in the twelfth house
g. ♄ in ♈ in the ninth house
h. ♅ in ♍ in the eighth house
i. ♆ in ♐ in the fifth house
j. ♇ in ♊ in the sixth house

1. Sociable and takes initiative in group activities. _____
2. Ambitious and vitally involved in the career. _____
3. Communicates powerfully in the daily work situation. _____
4. Obtains harmony and peace from philosophizing about the mystical. _____
5. Is emotionally and materially gratified by brothers and sisters. _____
6. Can develop philosophically and spiritually through one's children or confused by them. _____
7. Communication and mothering are important attributes of the personality. _____
8. Disciplined and aggressive in higher education. _____
9. Outgoing and affectionate with a partner. _____
10. Unusual but intensely emotional ideas about sex. _____

EXERCISE 54 Planets, Signs, Houses 8

Place the most appropriate letter next to each statement given below.

a. ☉ in ♓ in the sixth house
b. ☽ in ♑ in the fourth house
c. ☿ in ♒ in the ninth house
d. ♀ in ♍ in the eleventh house
e. ♂ in ♏ in the tenth house
f. ♃ in ♈ in the first house
g. ♄ in ♎ in the second house
h. ♅ in ♍ in the fifth house
i. ♆ in ♌ in the eighth house
j. ♇ in ♌ in the seventh house

1. Dramatically self-sacrificing in sex. _____
2. Enjoys serving humanitarian causes. _____
3. A forceful but jovial personality. _____
4. Strict but motherly in the home. _____
5. Is powerful and domineering in partnerships. _____
6. Deep-probing, persistent and intitiating in the career. _____
7. Receives ego gratification through being self-sacrificing in daily work. _____
8. May earn one's living through cataloguing works of art. _____
9. Has unusual children of whom the individual may be critical. _____
10. Original and clever when involved in higher education. _____

EXERCISES 55-58

This group of exercises deals with planets in aspect. When two planets are in aspect to each other their energies work together in some way. Although certain aspects have a "hard" quality, and others are "soft," they should not be understood as "bad" or "good." Therefore, the particular aspect is not mentioned. Sextiles, trines, quintiles, bi-quintiles and some conjunctions (depending on the planets involved) are considered "soft," while squares, oppositions, semi-squares, sesqui-quadrates, quincunxes and some conjunctions are considered "hard." It is impossible, however, to determine from the chart whether or not an individual is utilizing the energies positively or negatively. Someone with a square may have worked through the obstacles and successfully solved its problem, and someone with a trine may have experienced its negative energies because it is easier to do so. The descriptions given do not cover all possible meanings of the combinations.

EXERCISE 55   Planets in Aspect 1

Place the appropriate letter next to each description given below.
a. ☉ - ☿
b. ☉ - ♃
c. ☽ - ♅
d. ☽ - ♇
e. ☿ - ♅
f. ♀ - ♂
g. ♀ - ♄
h. ♂ - ♆
i. ♃ - ♄
j. ♆ - ♇

1. Analyzes the emotions deeply or feels the need to be in control of the emotions. _____
2. Expression of affection is difficult, or one is affectionate with older people. _____
3. Fatigues easily or initiates well in spiritual matters. _____
4. Expresses oneself optimistically or gives too much of the self. _____
5. Original thinker or erratic in expressing oneself verbally. _____
6. Is strongly spiritual and highly evolved or is confused when trying to probe deeply. _____
7. Has sex appeal or too aggressive in expressing one's affection. _____
8. Has an unusual mother, or emotions fluctuate radically and suddenly. _____
9. Uses the higher mind in an orderly way or is restricted in development of the higher mind. _____
10. Exercise of cleverness is an ego need, or one talks too energetically. _____

EXERCISE 56   Planets in Aspect 2

Place the appropriate letter next to each description given below.

a. ☉ - ♂
b. ☉ - ♄
c. ☽ - ♃
d. ☽ - ♆
e. ☿ - ♃
f. ☿ - ♄
g. ♀ - ♆
h. ♀ - ♇
i. ♂ - ♅
j. ♅ - ♇

1. Initiates with originality or is erratically aggressive. _____
2. Communicates a great deal or exaggerates in communications. _____
3. Works methodically toward satisfying ego needs, or vitality is restricted. _____
4. Emotions are expressed through spirituality, or the individual has a mother who is a martyr. _____
5. One has to solve a problem involving a need for power and a desire for independence, or one analyzes in an original way. _____
6. Has artistic ability or suffers in love. _____
7. Tremendous energy, or one expresses ego needs too aggressively. _____
8. Difficulty communicating or speaks in a logical and orderly manner. _____
9. Has great emotional capacity or is too emotional. _____
10. Feels affection deeply or must control love situations. _____

EXERCISE 57   Planets in Aspect 3

Place the appropriate letter next to each description given below.

a. ☉ - ☽
b. ☉ - ♀
c. ☽ - ♂
d. ☿ - ♀
e. ☿ - ♆

f. ♀ - ♅
g. ♂ - ♃
h. ♃ - ♅
i. ♄ - ♆
j. ♄ - ♇

1. Has writing ability or is lazy about communicating. _____
2. Falls in love suddenly or is erratic in love. _____
3. Is emotionally aggressive or energetically expresses the emotions. _____
4. Has a great deal of energy or initiates too aggressively. _____
5. Power is an ego need, or one deeply analyzes one's ego needs. _____
6. Communicates imaginatively or rationalizes. _____
7. One has original philosophical ideas or is erratic in the use of the higher mind. _____
8. Moody, or emotions are important for ego satisfaction. _____
9. The individual's imagination is stifled, or he applies spirituality practically. _____
10. Power is restricted, or one channels his power. _____

EXERCISE 58　　　　　　　Planets in Aspect 4

Place the appropriate letter next to each description given below.

a. ☉ - ♀　　　　　　f. ☿ - ♂
b. ☉ - ♅　　　　　　g. ♂ - ♄
c. ☉ - ♆　　　　　　h. ♂ - ♀
d. ☽ - ☿　　　　　　i. ♃ - ♆
e. ☽ - ♀　　　　　　j. ♄ - ♅

1. Has a quick mind or talks too rapidly. _____
2. Is very spiritual and philosophical or is confused by philsophical thought. _____
3. Receives ego gratification through spirituality or has a father who is confusing or absent. _____
4. Expresses emotions easily, or the emotions interfere with logical thinking. _____
5. Charming person or relies on charm for ego satisfaction. _____
6. Has tremendous energy or is physically violent. _____
7. Unusual ego needs or has a father who is a "free spirit." _____
8. Energies are restricted or one plans carefully before taking the initiative. _____
9. Originality restricted or kept within bounds. _____
10. Becomes emotionally involved easily in love relationships or is hesitant about becoming emotionally involved in romance. _____

EXERCISE 59   The Nodes

The Nodes of the Moon symbolize relationships. The North Node has the quality of Jupiter: it is what flows easily and shows how and where one grows and develops through associations; it is what one gets from others. The South Node is like Saturn: it indicates what must be worked on, and how and where one has lessons to learn through associations; it denotes our responsibility to others.

Since the two Nodes are always opposite each other, they should be treated as a unit; and, logically, growth and responsibility should both be part of any relationship.

The signs of the Nodes indicate general qualities of relationships; and in dealing with others the characteristics of both signs involved must be considered, even though at times they seem to conflict. (E.g., Aries-Libra, attraction to initiating or aggressive individuals and, yet, a need to share with others as well; Taurus-Scorpio, a need for material security but being drawn to others for emotional reasons also; etc.).

The houses in which the Nodes are posited show how the individual relates to others. (E.g., the first-seventh house, on a one-to-one basis; second-eighth house, on the material plane—one's resources, other people's resources, etc.)

Aspects between the Nodes and planets provide more specific features of relationships. The hard aspects denote obstacles that must be overcome or challenges that must be faced, and the soft aspects, what occurs easily; but any of these manifestations may be experienced as positive or negative. Therefore, the type of aspects is omitted from the following exercise, and the characterizations include both positive and negative qualities. There are other possible manifestations of the combinations given.

EXERCISE 59　　　　　　　　　Nodes in Aspect

Place the appropriate letter next to each characterization given below.

a. ☉ - ☊ ☋
b. ☽ - ☊ ☋
c. ☿ - ☊ ☋
d. ♀ - ☊ ☋
e. ♂ - ☊ ☋

f. ♃ - ☊ ☋
g. ♄ - ☊ ☋
h. ♅ - ☊ ☋
i. ♆ - ☊ ☋
j. ♇ - ☊ ☋

1. Deeply analyzes all relationships, or power plays an important role in relationships. _____
2. Sensitive to others and perhaps mothers them, or there is fluctuation in relationships. _____
3. Develops and grows through relating to others or gives too much of oneself. _____
4. Is attracted to spiritual people or is confused in associations. _____
5. Becomes involved in alliances for ego reasons or throws oneself whole-heartedly into alliances. _____
6. Enjoys relating to others or becomes romantically involved too easily in relationships. _____
7. Deals conscientiously and honestly with people or does not relate easily to them. _____
8. Likes active associations or may be too aggressive in association with others. _____
9. Communicates easily with others or talks too much in relationships. _____
10. Attracted to unusual people or begins and ends involvements suddenly. _____

61

EXERCISE 60　　　　　　　　　　MC in Aspect

The tenth house represents one's role in the world (including career); therefore, the Midheaven (MC), which is the cusp of the tenth house, indicates part of the impression we make on others. The sign on the MC denotes general characteristics, and planets in aspect to the MC show a specific quality that is ascribed to the individual by the world. Although the energies of the planets are strong, the manifestations may be positive or negative regardless of whether the aspect is "soft" or "hard." Therefore, the particular aspect is omitted. There are other possible manifestations of the combinations given.

Place the most appropriate letter next to each characterization given below.

a. ☉-MC
b. ☽-MC
c. ☿-MC
d. ♀-MC
e. ♂-MC
f. ♃-MC
g. ♄-MC
h. ♅-MC
i. ♆-MC
j. ♇-MC

1. Has charisma or seems confused. _____
2. Is an initiator or is aggressive. _____
3. Seen as a futuristic thinker or a non-conformist. _____
4. Appears to be moody or sensitive to the emotional needs of others. _____
5. Exudes charm or exhibits laziness. _____
6. Seems serious or inhibited. _____
7. Gives the impression of being an egotist or a warm and vital person. _____
8. Seen as a jovial, optimistic person or is overbearing. _____
9. Communicating is an essential part of one's role in the world, or one talks too much. _____
10. Seems profound and deeply analytical or gives the impression of being "power hungry." _____

EXERCISE 61   Ascendant in Aspect

The first house represents the personality; therefore, the sign of the Ascendant (the Ascendant being the cusp of the first house) indicates characteristics that are important in describing the personality. Planets in aspect to the Ascendant have an important influence on the personality. The influence may have positive or negative manifestations regardless of whether the aspect is "soft" or "hard." Therefore, the particular aspect is omitted. There are other possible manifestations of the combinations given.

Place the most appropriate letter next to each characterization given below.

a. ☉ -Asc.
b. ☽ -Asc.
c. ☿ -Asc.
d. ♀ -Asc.
e. ♂ -Asc.
f. ♃ -Asc.
g. ♄ -Asc.
h. ♅ -Asc.
i. ♆ -Asc.
j. ♇ -Asc.

1. Shy or has a strong sense of responsibility. _____
2. Charming and attractive or lazy. _____
3. Optimistic or tendency to be overweight. _____
4. The self is important, or one is warm-hearted. _____
5. Energetic or aggressive. _____
6. Moody or motherly. _____
7. Spiritual or confused. _____
8. Communications are an important function of the personality or talks too much. _____
9. Independent or eccentric. _____
10. Power over self or possible personality transformation during the lifetime. _____

EXERCISE 62   Major Configurations 1

Major configurations indicate patterns in the life and the *modus operandi* of the individual. Below are descriptions of the general way in which the configurations may be expressed. Place the most appropriate letter next to each description.

a. Grand Trine in fire
b. Grand Trine in earth
c. Grand Trine in air
d. Grand Trine in water
e. T-Square or Grand Cross in cardinal signs
f. T-Square or Grand Cross in fixed signs
g. T-Square or Grand Cross in mutable signs
h. Cradle
i. Yod

1. There will be a definite change at some point in the individual's life. _____
2. The individual has persistence to overcome obstacles or is stubborn. _____
3. The person communicates easily and deals well with abstract ideas but may rationalize. _____
4. Help will come from outside. The individual will be standing in the right place, at the right time, at some point in his life. _____
5. The person is very practical and may receive material gains during his lifetime but may be callous. _____
6. The native involves himself in situations that create problems and then has to extricate himself. _____
7. The individual is warm, enthusiastic and outgoing but may over-extend himself. _____
8. The native is sympathetic and intuitive but may be ruled by his emotions. _____
9. The individual is adaptable and changeable. When obstacles or problems appear, there can be a floundering from one decision to another. _____

EXERCISE 63 — Major Configurations 2

In major configurations the energies of the planets and points work together, but the manifestations may be positive or negative. Below, four major configurations and two possible descriptions for each configuration are given. Place the appropriate letter next to each description.

a. ☉ ☽ ♄
b. ☽ ☿ Asc.
c. ♀ ♅ ♆
d. ♂ ♃ ♇

1. The individual has artistic talent and expresses it with great originality. _____
2. The native is too emotional when communicating about himself. _____
3. This individual has the power to initiate great and beneficial plans. _____
4. The person falls in love easily and is deceived in love relationships. _____
5. Ego needs of the individual are restricted, and emotions controlled too much. _____
6. Common sense and intuition are important attributes of the personality. _____
7. The individual uses violence to acquire power. _____
8. This person expresses ego and emotional needs in a disciplined way. _____

EXERCISE 64

Major Configurations 3

Below four major configurations and two possible descriptions for each configuration are given. Place the most appropriate letter to each description.

a. ☉ ♀ MC
b. ☿ ♃ ♆
c. ☽ ♀ Asc.
d. ♂ ♄ ♅

1. The individual has a sensitive and charming personality. _____

2. The person receives ego satisfaction through exercising great power in the career. _____

3. The native combines initiative with originality in a disciplined manner. _____

4. The individual writes a great deal and with tremendous imagination. _____

5. The native may tend to exaggerate and deceive in communications. _____

6. The person may use his vital energy ruthlessly in the world. _____

7. Moodiness and laziness may be attributes of the personality. _____

8. The initiative of this individual may be sporadic and sometimes totally inhibited. _____

EXERCISE 65 **Major Configurations 4**

Below, four major configurations and two possible descriptions for each configuration are given. Place the most appropriate letter next to each description.

a. ☉ ♂ ♆
b. ☽ ♅ MC
c. ♀ ♂ ♃
d. ☿ ♄ ♇

1. This person communicates in a disciplined, powerful manner. _____
2. The individual utilizes originality in dealing with the public through his career. _____
3. The native masks his aggressiveness with charm and joviality. _____
4. The vital energy and initiative of this indiviual may be drained. _____
5. The individual demonstrates courage and receives ego gratification when being self-sacrificing. _____
6. This native may deal with the world in an emotional and erratic way. _____
7. The person has charm and a great deal of sex appeal. _____
8. The articulateness of this individual may be restricted because of introspection. _____

EXERCISE 66 — Major Configurations 5

Below, four major configurations and two possible descriptions for each configuration are given. Place the most appropriate letter next to each description.

a. ☉ ♃ ♅
b. ☿ ♂ ♆

c. ♀ ♄ ♀
d. ☽ ♀ MC

1. This individual wields power over the public in his career. _____

2. The ego is gratified through great independence. _____

3. The native is analytical about love relationships, and display of affection is restricted. _____

4. This person is energetic and imaginative in speaking and writing. _____

5. The individual creates powerful, yet structured, works of art. _____

6. Vital energy is expressed in a jovial and original manner. _____

7. Emotional sensitivity and deep analytical ability are utilized in the career. _____

8. The individual is aggressive and cleverly deceptive. _____

INTRODUCTION TO CHART INTERPRETATION

Thus far the exercises have included integration of two signs, then three; signs in houses; planets in houses; planets in signs and houses; planets and points in aspects and major configurations. The final section, by delineating actual charts, will apply and expand upon the principles introduced previously.

When integrating various components in an actual interpretation, it is best first to ascribe key words to all of the factors, and then to convert these key words into a meaningful description of the individual. Let us examine Henry Kissinger in this manner.

The signs stressed are Gemini (Sun, Ascendant, stellium and emphasis by signs), then Libra (Moon), Pisces (twelfth house stellium) and Sagittarius (emphasis by house). Since Gemini is so strongly represented, the characteristics of this sign will be very evident. Consider such Gemini words as mutable, adaptable, gregarious, sociable, communicative, mental. Since Pisces and Sagittarius are also mutable signs, mutability and adaptability are reinforced. Libra, like Gemini, is an air sign; therefore communications and use of the mind are further supported. Pisces also adds emotionality (water) and compassion. Sagittarius supplies enthusiasm (fire) and an interest in development and growth, foreign affairs and higher education. Libra indicates a need for harmony and an interest in others on a close one-to-one basis. Other factors, such as a Grand Trine in air and another in water, could be incorporated for a more complete delineation, but employing only the signs mentioned a description of Henry Kissinger could be the following.

Henry Kissinger is a sociable (Gemini) and adaptable (Gemini, Sagittarius and Pisces) individual who enjoys using his mind and communicating with others (Gemini and Libra). His interest in other people includes consideration of someone else's point of view (Libra) and deep feeling (Pisces) for those with whom he deals. Since he is adaptable (Gemini, Sagittarius and Pisces) he can utilize input from those with whom he socializes (Gemini) and communicates (Gemini and Libra) to broaden himself (Sagittarius) and attain harmony (Libra).

Major configurations can be handled in a similar way. Key words for the aspects, elements or modes, and the planets and points provide a basis for an integrated interpretation of the patterns. The houses in which the planets and points are posited and the houses which the planets rule indicate areas where the pattern will most likely be overtly manifested.

Henry Kissinger
May 27, 1923
05:30 Hrs. C.E.T.
Furth, Germany

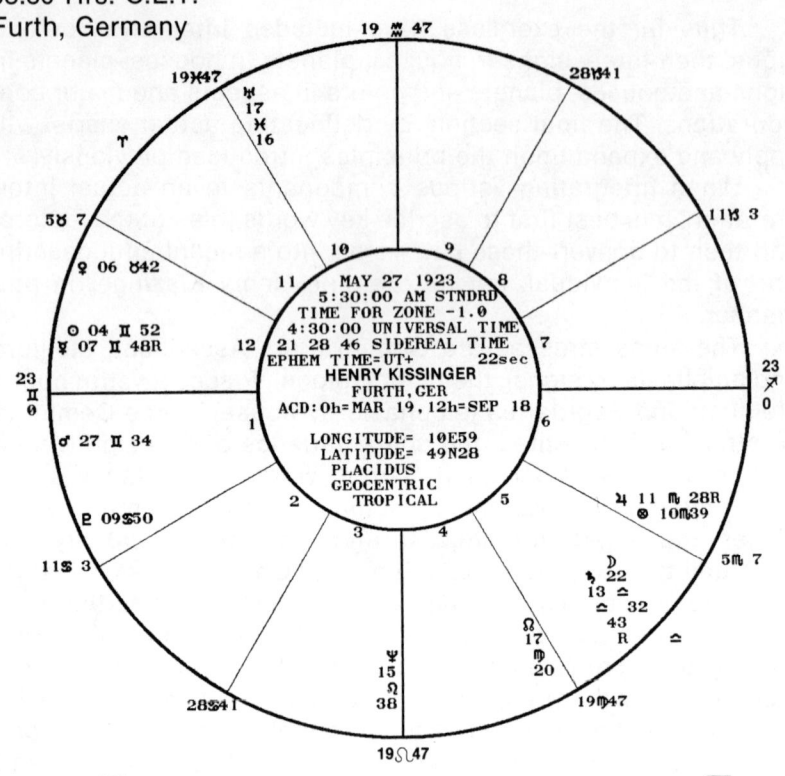

		by Sign	by House
Elements:	Fire	♆	♂♀♄☽
	Earth	♀	♃♅
	Air	☉☿A♂♄☽MC	♆
	Water	♀♃♅	♀☉☿
Modes:	Cardinal	♀♄☽	♂♀♅
	Fixed	♀♆♃MC	♄☽
	Mutable	☉☿A♂♅	♆♃♀☉☿
Sign Emphasis:		♊	♐

Sun ♊ Moon ♎ Ascendant ♊
Stelliums ♊, 12th house (♓)

70

Henry Kissinger

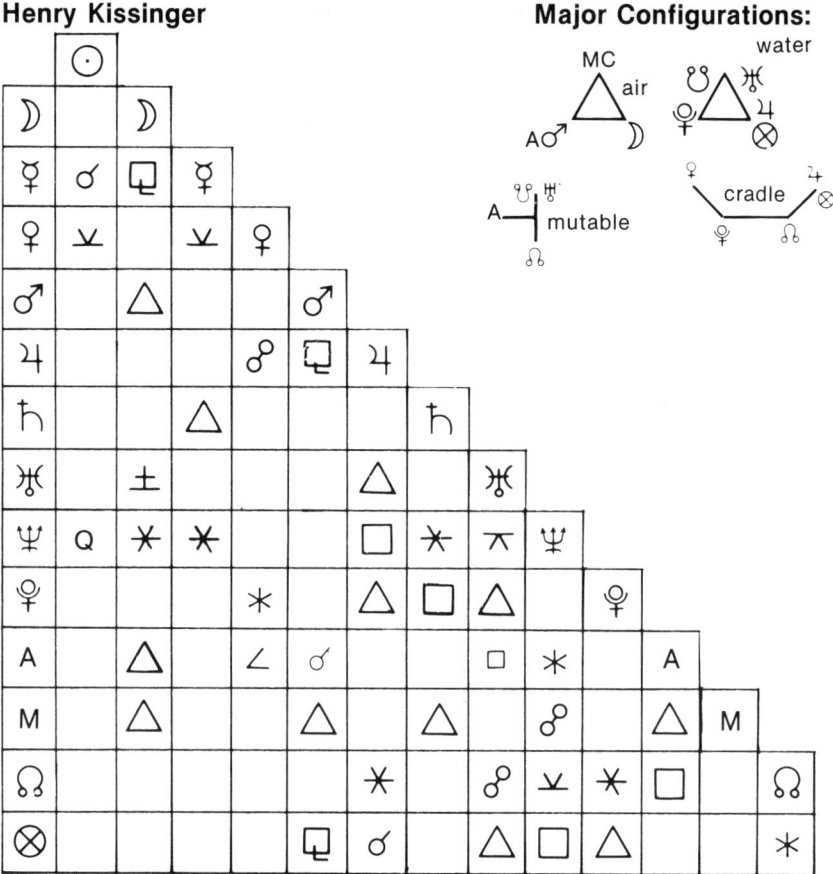

The most heavily emphasized sign is Gemini (Sun, Ascendant, stellium and emphasis by sign). Libra (Moon, Pisces (twelfth house stellium) and Sagittarius (emphasis by house) follow in importance and should be incorporated into an overall synthesis after the first sign is interpreted.

The major configurations are a Grand Trine in air (MC trine Ascendant conjunct Mars; trine Moon), a Grand Trine in water (Uranus conjunct South Node; trine Jupiter conjunct Part of Fortune; trine Pluto), a mutable T-Square (Uranus conjunct South Node, opposition North Node, square Ascendant) and a Cradle (Venus sextile Pluto; sextile North Node; sextile Jupiter conjunct Part of Fortune).

The orbs I have used are 8° for major aspects (conjunction, sextile, square, trine and opposition) and 2° for minor aspects (semi-sextile, semi-square, quintile, sesqui-quadrate, bi-quintile and quincunx).

71

Introduction to Chart Interpretation

One of the major configurations is a Grand Trine in water, consisting of Uranus conjunct the South Node, trine Jupiter conjunct the Part of Fortune, trine Pluto. Trines are soft aspects, and a Grand Trine is indicative of what flows easily. Water represents emotions and intuition. Among the key words for the planets involved are sudden action or creative thinking for Uranus, complex thinking and great plans for Jupiter, and power and deep analysis for Pluto. The South Node is part of the relationship axis and has the quality of Saturn, so it can denote discipline and responsibility. The Part of Fortune signifies a sense of wholeness or fulfillment. Thus, the configuration might be described as follows:

Kissinger can easily utilize his intuition (Grand Trine in water) to analyze (Pluto) complex situations (Jupiter) creatively (Uranus) and responsibly (South Node) to provide self-fulfillment (Part of Fortune). His personality (Pluto in the first house) will play a direct role in the process and may be prominent in his career (Uranus and South Node in the tenth house, and Uranus co-ruling the tenth house) or as part of his daily work routine (Jupiter and Part of Fortune in the sixth house, and Pluto co-ruling the sixth house). His career also may involve others (South Node) on a one-to-one basis (Jupiter ruling the seventh house) or groups (Jupiter co-ruling the eleventh house).

He also has a mutable T-Square, including the South Node conjunct Uranus, opposition the North Node, square the Ascendant. Squares and oppositions are hard aspects. Squares involve obstacles or problems that must be faced, and oppositions show a need to balance; therefore, the T-Square indicates situations that must be worked on. Mutability implies flexibility, fluctuation and the possibility that others create the problems (the Node axis further suggests that the problems come from others). Uranus again is sudden change; the Node axis involves relationships; and the Ascendant draws in the personality.

Therefore, Kissinger may have problems in relationships (Node axis), often coming from others (mutable T-Square). Relationships may change suddenly (Uranus conjunct South Node, and mutable T-Square) especially when the forcefulness of the personality is an important factor (Ascendant squares Nodes and Uranus). These problems may emerge in the career (Uranus conjunct South Node in the tenth house, and Uranus co-ruling the tenth house), at home (North Node in the fourth house), or at any

Introduction to Chart Interpretation

time when the personality (Ascendant) plays a major part in these areas.

There is a Grand Trine in air as well in this chart. This Grand Trine involves the MC, the Ascendant, Mars and the Moon. A Grand Trine in air denotes facility with communications and other basic mental functions. The Ascendant is again the personality; Mars is aggressive initiative; the MC is the career or role in the world; and the Moon represents the public or responsiveness.

Communications flow easily (Grand Trine in air, and the Moon ruling the third house of communications) and creatively (Moon in the fifth house of creativity) when the personality (Ascendant) is aggressively (Mars) responding (Moon) to the public (Moon) through the career (MC). Of course, there is the possibility of overaggressiveness.

The final major configuration in Kissinger's chart is a Cradle, consisting of Venus sextile Pluto, sextile the North Node, sextile a conjunction of Jupiter and the Part of Fortune. (Thus, Venus and the North Node are also trine;* Pluto and Jupiter/Part of Fortune are trine; and Venus and Jupiter/Part of Fortune are in opposition). The configuration therefore contains three sextiles, two trines and one opposition.

A Cradle represents opportunities coming from others. It is basically soft (sextiles and trines), but the individual has to determine whether or not to utilize the opportunity and must balance it (opposition) in his life. Kissinger might be offered pleasure (Venus), expansion (Jupiter) and personal fulfillment (Part of Fortune) through power (Pluto) in relationships (North Node). This opportunity could occur in, or affect, a number of areas. For instance, it could involve the daily work situation (Jupiter and the Part of Fortune in the sixth house and Pluto co-ruling it) in institutions or behind the scenes (Venus in the twelfth house and ruling it) and affect the personality (Pluto in the first house), the home (North Node in the fourth house) and one-to-one relationships (Jupiter ruling the seventh house).

The major configurations are interconnected in various ways, indicating a combination of difficulty and ease—a kind of balance astrologers hope to find in a chart. Therefore, there are alternatives to the handling of problems and enough restraint to control the soft aspects. All of the foregoing could be more fully

*In major configurations I sometimes extend the orb.

Introduction to Chart Interpretation

explained and expanded, but it is the **process** of delineation, not a **complete** interpretation, that is being presented here.

In examining the particular areas of a life, a simple method of integration can be utilized. Start with key words for the signs contained in the appropriate house; next, note planets and points in the house for more definite requirements in the area. Aspects and major configurations connected with these planets and points will provide more information, including what will flow easily in these areas and what types of problems are likely to arise; and finally, house placement of the ruler or co-rulers and their aspects complete the picture.

For example, let us investigate Henry Kissinger's profession (tenth house). The signs contained in the house are Aquarius and Pisces. Aquarius is an air sign and indicates that communications and use of the mind are stressed in the career. It is also the sign of humanitarian idealism, impersonal detachment, originality and independence. Pisces adds emotionality, compassion, flexibility and self-sacrifice. There are a number of ways these signs could be combined. One would be that Henry Kissinger would need a career involving humanitarian causes. He might try to help others in an impersonal manner, but inevitably there would be emotional involvement as well. Professionally he should have enough independence to utilize his originality and his creative mind. He would undoubtedly choose a career in which he could help others.

Uranus and the South Node in the tenth house support the above themes. Uranus substantiates the idea that he needs independence in his career and will exercise originality. It also indicates that he might suddenly change professions but most likely would substitute one humanitarian profession for another. The South Node not only reemphasizes the need for dealing with others through his work, but also having a Saturnian quality, adds a sense of responsibility for those with whom he comes into contact professionally.

As the aspects and configurations containing Uranus and the South Node are noted, it becomes obvious that some facets of the career will flow easily and others will require effort. The mutable T-Square could be directly manifested in this area by the personality (Ascendant) interfering with professional relationships (Nodes and the tenth house) suddenly and sporadically

Introduction to Chart Interpretation

(Uranus and the mutability); sudden changes (Uranus) in professional relationships (Nodes and the tenth house) could have a detrimental effect on the personality (Ascendant) and make him indecisive (mutable T-Square). These potential problems, however, could be alleviated or avoided by activating the Grand Trine in water which connects to the T-Square through Uranus conjunct the South Node, and which includes a trine of these points to Pluto and Jupiter. Through exercising intuition (water) and great (Jupiter) power (Pluto), fluctuation and other relationship problems could be kept within appropriate limits. The individual aspects from other planets and points provide further alternatives for action or show specific types of difficulties that might occur.

Finally, the placement of the tenth house co-rulers and their aspects inform us that career is emphasized (Uranus in the tenth house); and support the theme that Kissinger must be creative in his career (Saturn in the fifth house of creativity). The Uranus aspects have already been covered. The Saturn aspects reinforce some of the ideas previously mentioned and also supply some new information. The trine to Mercury reiterates the need to communicate and to use the mind in the career, and indicates that this need can be fulfilled in an orderly manner (Saturn) with ease (trine). The trine to the MC repeats the sense of professional (MC) responsibility (Saturn). And the sextile to Neptune corroborates the use of intuition and compassion. The square to Pluto, however, inhibits the use of raw power or force.

We could elaborate further by considering the signs in which the planets and points are positioned. Sometimes, too, an area is described by two or more houses. For instance, we have examined the career through the tenth house, but the sixth house describes the daily routine, and the second house shows how one earns a living. Therefore, we could investigate these houses for a more detailed description of the profession. We will concentrate, however, on a single house since the emphasis here is on learning a procedure rather than on developing a total interpretation.

Exercises 67-75 represent delineations of three charts for which the student should select the most appropriate interpretations. In exercises 70-75 career, partnership and the home are delineated. Each area is divided into two exercises since there are so many factors to consider, but all of the material would be combined in a total interpretation.

The lower case letters which appear in the descriptions indicate that a new factor is being introduced. This format simplifies

Introduction to Chart Interpretation

the organization of both the delineation and the answer sections.

The remainder of the exercises (76-99) afford the student the opportunity to create his own interpretations. In each chart three houses will examined, with one description offered for each exercise. Every house, however, represents numerous departments of life. In some cases the particular house will be delineated twice with different interpretations. The answer section gives one possibility, so that, as with all the exercises, there are other alternatives. The student's paragraph might differ from the writer's, but there should be enough similarity to recognize that the same signs, houses, planets, points and aspects are being discussed.

SAMPLE PRACTICE CHARTS

for Exercises 67-75

Chart A.

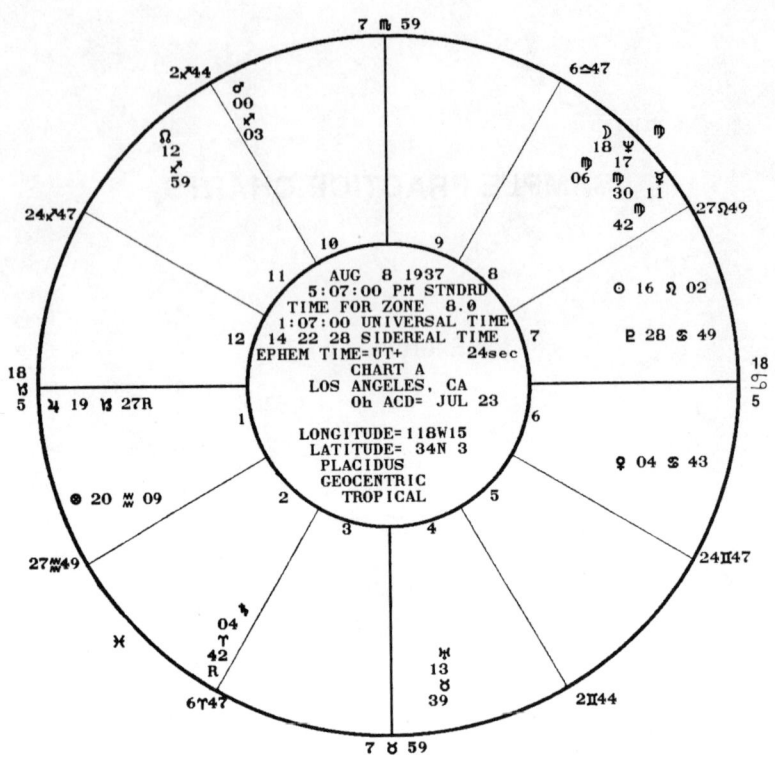

Sun ♌	**Moon** ♍	**Ascendant** ♑	
Stelliums ♍, 8th house			

		by Sign	by House
Elements:	Fire	♄ ☉ ♂	♃
	Earth	♅ ☿ ♆ ☽ A ♃	♄ ♀ ♂
	Air		♀ ☉
	Water	♀ ♇ MC	♅ ☿ ♆ ☽
Modes:	Cardinal	♄ ♀ ♇ A ♃	♃ ♅ ♇ ☉ ♂
	Fixed	♅ ☉ MC	♄ ☿ ♆ ☽
	Mutable	☿ ♆ ☽ ♂	♀
Sign Emphasis:		♑	♎

78

Chart A   **Major Configurations:**

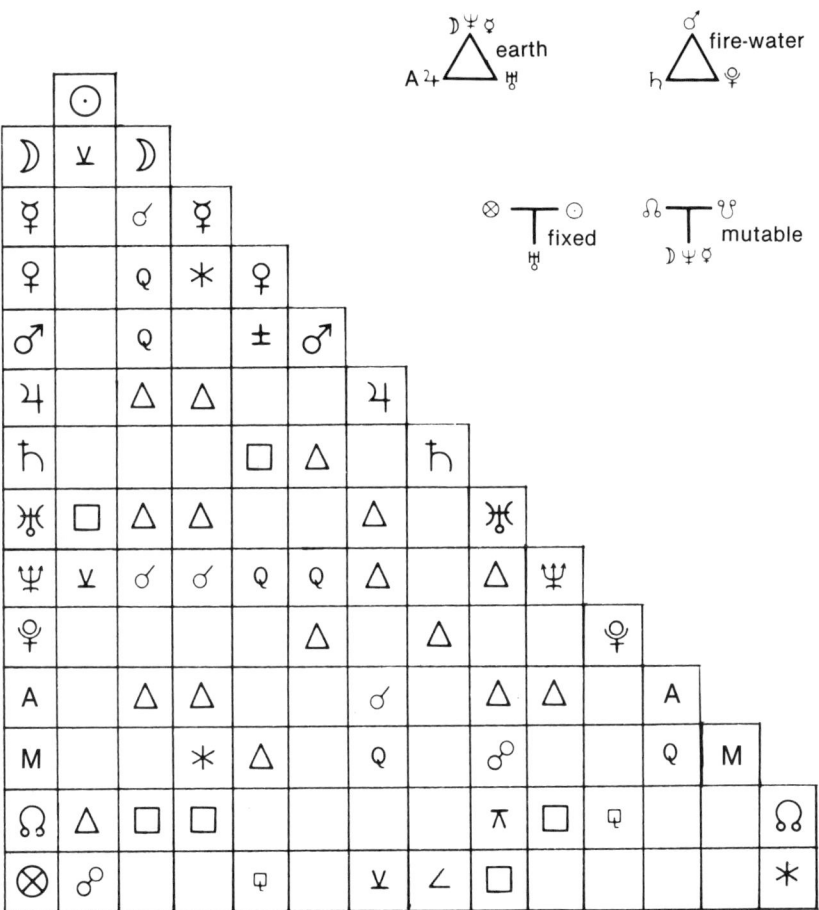

The most heavily emphasized signs are Virgo (Moon and stellium) and Capricorn (Ascendant and emphasis by sign). Leo (Sun), Scorpio (eighth house stellium) and Cancer (emphasis by house) follow in importance and should be incorporated into an overall synthesis after the first two signs are integrated.

The major configurations are a Grand Trine in earth (Ascendant conjunct Jupiter, trine Uranus, trine Mercury conjunct Neptune and Moon), a Grand Trine in fire and water (Saturn trine Pluto, trine Mars), a mutable T-Square (the Node axis square Mercury conjunct Neptune and Moon), and a fixed T-Square (Part of Fortune opposition Sun, square Uranus).

79

Chart B

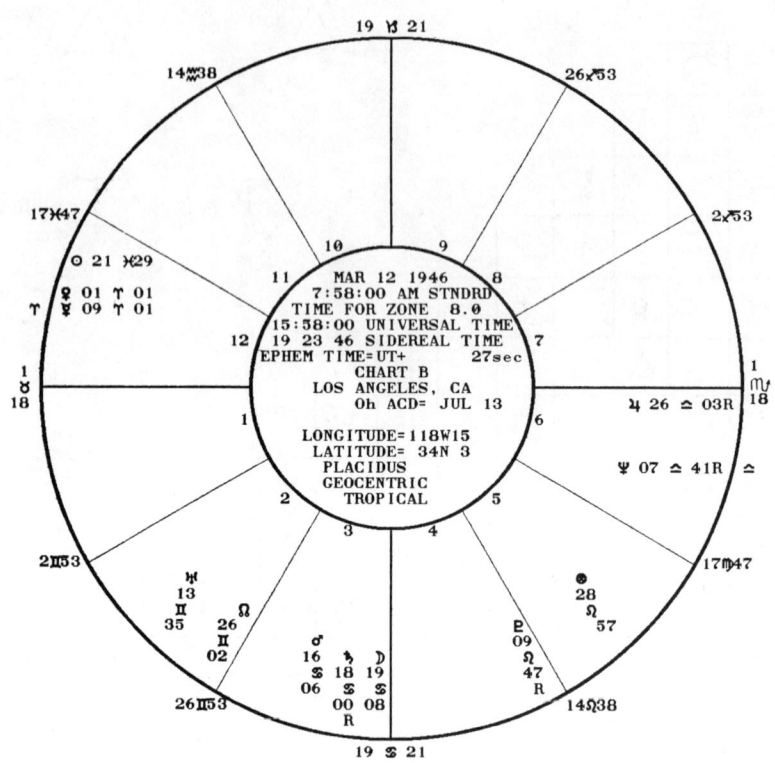

		by Sign	by House
Elements:	Fire	♀ ☿ ♀	
	Earth	A MC	♅ ♆ ♃
	Air	♅ ♆ ♃	♂ ♄ ☽
	Water	♂ ♄ ☽ ☉	♀ ☉ ☿
Modes:	Cardinal	♀ ☿ ♂ ♄ ☽ ♆ ♃ MC	♀
	Fixed	A ♀	♅
	Mutable	♅ ☉	♂ ♄ ☽ ♆ ♃ ☉ ☿
Sign Emphasis:		♋	♓

Sun ♓ Moon ♋ Ascendant ♉
Stelliums ♋, 3rd house-12th house

Chart B   **Major Configurations:**

The most heavily emphasized signs are Cancer (Moon, stellium and emphasis by sign) and Pisces (Sun, 12th house stellium and emphasis by house). Taurus (Ascendant) and Gemini (3rd house stellium) follow in importance and should be incorporated into an overall synthesis after the first two signs are integrated.

Major configurations include three T-Squares: one cardinal (MC opposition Saturn and Moon, square Jupiter*), one mutable (Sun square the Nodes) and one mutable-cardinal (Venus square the Nodes). There is also a Cradle (Mercury sextile Uranus, sextile Pluto, sextile Neptune).

*Saturn is slightly out of orb of a square to Jupiter, but the Moon, which is closely conjunct Saturn, is within orb.

81

Chart C

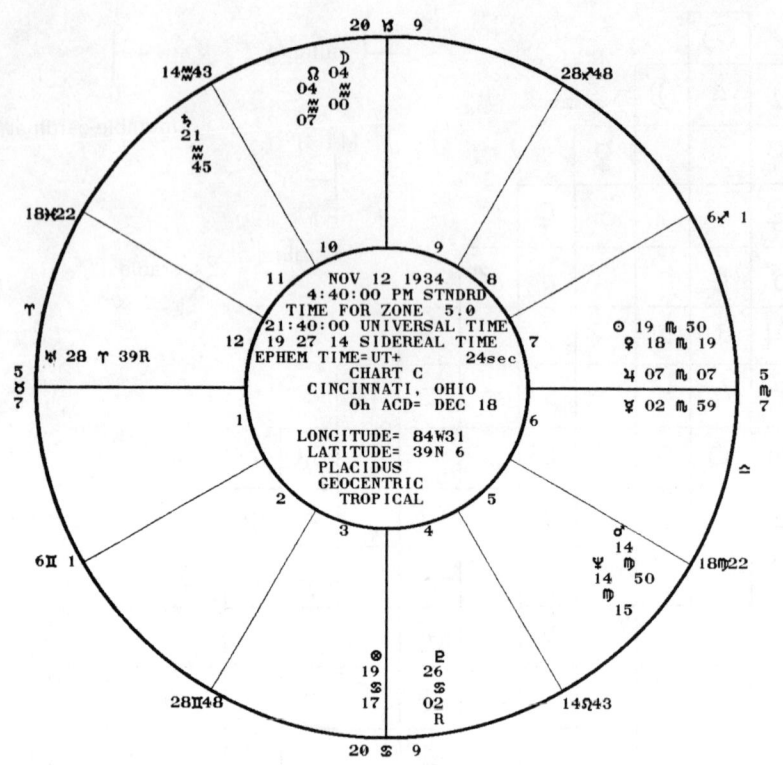

Sun ♏ **Moon** ♒ **Ascendant** ♉

Stelliums ♏, 7th house ♒

	by Sign	by House
Elements: Fire	♅	♆ ♂
Earth	♆ ♂ MC A	☿ ☽
Air	☽ ♄	♃ ♀ ☉ ♄
Water	♇ ☿ ♃ ♀ ☉	♇ ♅
Modes: Cardinal	♅ ♇ MC	♇ ♃ ♀ ☉ ☽
Fixed	☿ ♃ ♀ ☉ ☽ ♄ A	♆ ♂ ♄
Mutable	♆ ♂	☿ ♅
Sign Emphasis:	♏	♎

82

Chart C   **Major Configurations:**

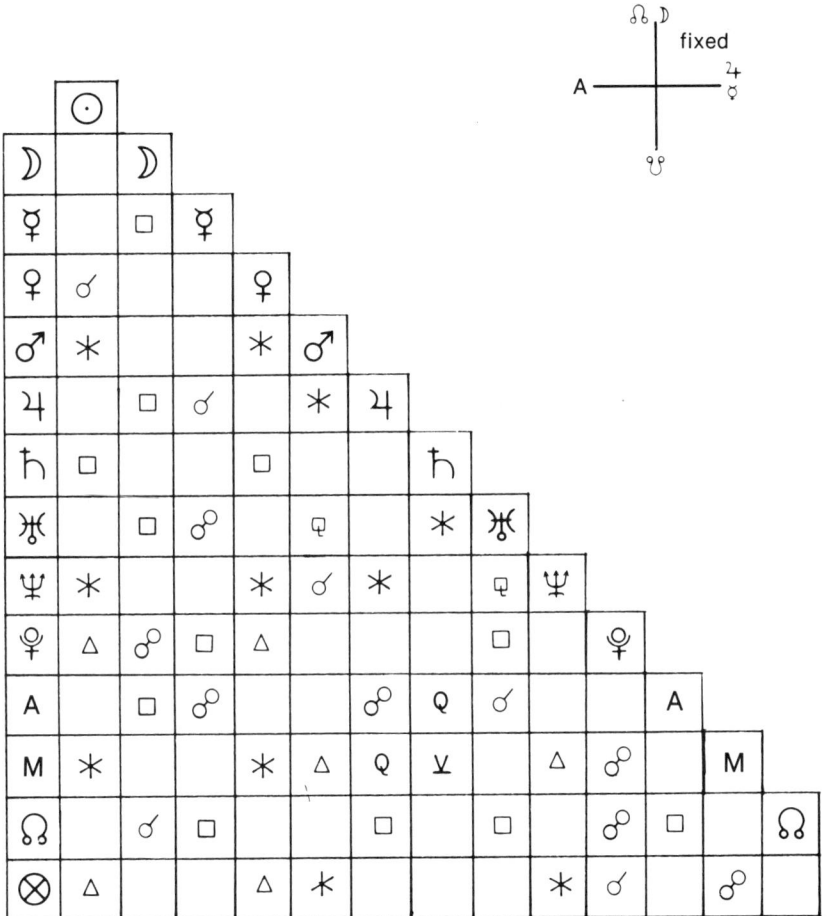

The most heavily emphasized signs are Scorpio (Sun, stellium and emphasis by sign). Aquarius (Moon and stellium) and Libra (emphasis by house and 7th house stellium). Taurus (Ascendant) follows in importance and should be incorporated into an overall synthesis after the first three signs are integrated.

There is one major configuration, a fixed Grand Cross, which includes a great deal of the chart (Moon conjunct North Node, opposition South Node, square Ascendant square a conjunction of Mercury and Jupiter). Uranus is conjunct the Ascendant which, using a wider orb, squares Pluto conjunct the South Node.

EXERCISE 67 — Chart Interpretation 1

A. Chart A— ♍ and ♑ with ♌, ♏ and ♋
B. Chart B— ♋ and ♓ with ♉ and ♊
C. Chart C— ♏, ♒ and ♎ with ♉

1. This individual is highly emotional, compassionate and protective and needs understanding and mothering. Soft and gently emotionality is accompanied by sociability and adaptability. He or she might be self-sacrificing at times but the self-sacrifice is tempered by a degree of practicality. When a goal or material gain is involved there is the ability to strive persistently to attain it. _____
2. This person is hard-driving, persistent and emotional. There is a need for close one-to-one relationships, and the emotionality may manifest itself as possessiveness in intimate involvements. There is an urge to share with a partner on the one hand, but there is also the desire to receive material rewards from others, to remain impersonal and independent, and to keep a great deal secret. _____
3. This native is basically practical, ambitious and career-oriented. He or she may be critical and give considerable attention to details. Underlying the practicality, however, are strong emotions which will manifest themselves in both a protective and self-protective manner. There is also the ability to be warm and outgoing. This person enjoys being the center of attention and will perform on stage or in the world. The deeper feelings, however, will not always be easily expressed. _____

EXERCISE 68   Chart Interpretation 2

Below two manifestations (one positive, one negative) of some of the major configurations are given. There are, or course. other possibilities. Place the appropriate letter next to each statement.

A. Chart A—mutable T-Square: North Node (☊) opposition South Node (☋), square a conjunction of Moon (☽), Neptune (♆) and Mercury (☿)
B. Chart A—fire-water Grand Trine: Saturn (♄) trine Mars (♂), trine Pluto (♀)
C. Chart A—earth Grand Trine: Ascendant conjunct Jupiter (♃), trine Uranus (♅), trine the conjunction of Mercury (☿), Neptune (♆) and Moon (☽)
D. Chart B—mutable T-Square: North Node (☊) opposition South Node (☋), square the Sun (☉)

1. People are sometimes drawn to this individual because of his or her vitality. _____

2. Originality, a pleasing personality—perhaps even charisma—are instrumental in obtaining material rewards. _____

3. Adaptable in relationships and can communicate well because of intuition and emotional sensitivity. _____
4. Obtains power through disciplined action. _____
5. Ego needs may sometimes be an asset and sometimes a detriment in relationships. _____
6. Can manipulate the public to gain personal pleasure and material rewards through unusual cleverness. _____
7. Emotional need for power and control can lead to violent action. _____
8. Relationships dissolve because the individual is too emotional and too clever. _____

EXERCISE 69 — Chart Interpretation 3

Below two manifestations (one positive, one negative) of some of the major configurations are given. There are, of course, other possibilities. Place the appropriate letter next to each statement.

A. Chart B—cardinal T-Square—MC opposition Saturn (♄) conjunct Moon (☽), square Jupiter (♃)
B. Chart B—mutable-cardinal T-Square—North Node (☊) opposition South Node (☋), square Venus (♀)
C. Chart C—fixed Grand Cross—Ascendant opposition Jupiter (♃) conjunct Mercury (☿), square North Node (☊) conjunct Moon (☽) on one side and South Node (☋) on the other

1. Displays an optimistic personality in communicating with the public or in relationships generally. _____
2. Emotions might interfere with development in the career. _____
3. Charm furthers the individual in associations. _____
4. Could repeatedly manipulate relationships through a strong personality which utilizes emotional appeal and makes grand promises in conversation. _____
5. Emotions are disciplined for advancement in the career. _____
6. Self-indulgent in associations. _____

EXERCISE 70   Chart Interpretation 4

Career (Tenth House)

Place the appropriate letter next to each description given below.

A. Chart A—**Signs in the 10th house**: Scorpio (♏) and Sagittarius (♐)
Planets and points in the house:* Mars (♂)
Major configurations and aspects to the planets and points in the house: Mars (♂) is part of a fire-water Grand Trine with Saturn (♄) and Pluto (♀); Mars (♂) is also quintile Moon (☽) and Neptune (♆) and bi-quintile Venus (♀).

B. Chart B—**Signs in the 10th house**: Capricorn (♑) and Aquarius (♒)
Planets and points in the house:* None
Major configurations and aspects to the planets and points in the house: None

C. Chart C—**Signs in the 10th House**: Capricorn (♑) and Aquarius (♒) **Planets and points in the house:*** Moon (☽) and North Node (☊)
Major configurations and aspects to the planets and points in the house: Moon (☽) and North Node (☊), closely conjunct and part of a fixed Grand Cross, are opposite South Node (☋), square Ascendant on the one side and Mercury (☿) conjunct Jupiter (♃) on the other; also Moon (☽) and North Node (☊) are square Uranus (♅) and opposition Pluto (♀).**

1. (a) Discipline and material security are requirements for the career, but the need for independence and freedom must be accommodated as well. (b) There are a number of indications that this individual should relate to others through his or her profession. (c) Emotions, forcefulness and exaggerated promises could all be identified with the personality and expressed through the career. (d) This individual, however, would communicate powerfully, effectively and with originality in this area. _____

2. (a) A career should include deep-probing analysis and contribute to the growth of the individual. Other people's resources could be utilized as well. (b) Taking initiative on the job is important, and this would be done with enthusiasm

*Although the MC is the cusp of the tenth house and not in it, aspects and major configurations involving the MC would affect the career. For the sake of simplicity, however, these are omitted.
**In conjunctions where one planet is within orb of an aspect and the other is slightly out of orb, I allow a larger orb.

EXERCISE 70 **Chart Interpretation 4**

and zeal. (c) This initiative would combine easily with discipline and power, and (d) there are a number of indications that this person could be an executive or a leader in his profession. (e) The use of intuition, sensitivity and charm would be an asset to the career. _____
3. (a) This individual will be hard-working and disciplined in the career. (b) There is, however, a need for creativity and independence there as well. (c) Although the individual has the ability to work hard and long to get ahead, (d) behavior may be erratic at times in this area. (e) He or she should direct career activities, (f) work alone or (g) combine efforts with others on an equal basis; but (h) would feel stifled if creativity were too closely directed. _____

EXERCISE 71   Chart Interpretation 5

Career (Tenth House)

Place the appropriate letter next to each description given below.

A. Chart A—**House placement of ruler of co-rulers**: Mars (♂) in the tenth house and Pluto (♀) in the seventh house

Major configurations and aspects to the ruler of co-rulers: Mars (♂) is part of a fire-water Grand Trine with Saturn (♄) and Pluto (♀) and is also quintile Moon (☽) and Neptune (♆) and bi-quintile Venus (♀); Pluto (♀) is part of a fire-water Grand Trine with Saturn (♄) and Mars (♂) and is also sesqui-quadrate North Node (☊).

B. Chart B—**House placement of ruler or co-rulers**: Saturn (♄) in the third house

Major configurations and aspects to the ruler or co-rulers: Saturn (♄), part of a cardinal T-Square, is conjunct Moon (☽), opposition MC and square Jupiter (♃); it is also conjunct Mars (♂) and trine Sun (☉).

C. Chart C—**House placement of ruler or co-rulers**: Saturn (♄) in the eleventh house

Major configurations and aspects to the ruler or co-rulers: Saturn (♄) squares Sun (☉) and Venus (♀), sextiles Uranus (♅), quintiles Ascendant and semi-sextiles MC.

1. (a) Communications are an important part of the career, and (b) the vital energy of the individual is easily expressed through it. (c) There might be great emotional outbursts because of the career, or (d) the emotions could be energetically expressed to expand the profession. _____

2. (a) Career is exceptionally important and will entail relations with others on a close one-to-one basis or with the public generally. (b) Power, initiative and discipline will flow easily together through the profession. (c) Charm, charisma and sensitivity to the emotional needs of others would be aggressively expressed in the career. (d) The need for power in the profession may cause problems in relationships but can be controlled through discipline. _____

3. (a) Career could involve working with groups or for humanitarian causes. (b) An evident charm generally may be restrained or limited in the career, but (c) discipline and order in the profession can add strength to the personality. (d) The individual can, however, utilize originality in the career, or behavior may be erratic there, and (e) restraint is needed. _____

EXERCISE 72   Chart Interpretation 6

Partnership (Seventh House)

Place the appropriate letter next to each description given below.

A. Chart A—**Signs in the 7th house**: Cancer (♋) and Leo (♌)
Planets and points in the house: Pluto (♇) and Sun (☉)
Major configurations and aspects to the planets and points in the house: Pluto (♇) is part of a fire-water Grand Trine with Mars (♂) and Saturn (♄), and is also sesqui-quadrate North Node (☊); Sun (☉), part of a fixed T-Square, is opposition Part of Fortune (⊗) and square Uranus (♅) and is also semi-sextile Moon (☾)* and Neptune (♆) and trine North Node (☊).

B. Chart B—**Signs in the 7th house**: Scorpio (♏) and Sagittarius (♐)
Planets and points in the house: None
Major configurations and aspects to the planets and points in the house: None

C. Chart C—**Signs in the 7th house**: Scorpio (♏) and Sagittarius (♐)
Planets and points in the house: Jupiter (♃), Venus (♀) and Sun (☉)
Major configurations and aspects to the planets and points in the house: Jupiter (♃) part of a fixed Grand Cross, is conjunct Mercury (☿), opposition Ascendant, and square North Node (☊) and Moon (☾) on one side and South Node (☋) on the other, and is also sextile Mars (♂) and Neptune (♆) and quintile MC; Sun (☉) is conjunct Venus (♀), square Saturn (♄), sextile Mars (♂), Neptune (♆) and MC and trine Pluto (♇) and Part of Fortune (⊗).

1. (a) Basic requirements for the partner would be someone to mother and protect or someone who was motherly and protective. Strong and tender feelings would be present. (b) There is also a need for a warm, outgoing partner who might like to be the center of attention or, more likely in this case, (c) a partner who would enjoy watching the native be the center of attention. (d) There are indications that this individual is the dominant partner and that this dominance would occur easily. (e) The dominance might cause problems in other relationships. (f) The individual can throw himself or herself wholeheartedly into partnerships, however, and satisfy ego needs and obtain a sense of fulfillment through

---

*The Moon's conjunction to Neptune pulls the Moon into the semi-sextile to the Sun.

EXERCISE 72   Chart Interpretation 6

partnerships as well. (g) Behavior may change suddenly in this area so that the individual will at times seem soft and sensitive. (h) Then all relationships will run smoothly. _____

2. (a) Deep emotionality and possibly possessiveness are evident in partnerships. (b) There is also a need for a partner who can help the individual develop and grow, or whom the native can help grow. (c) Great pleasure, personal fulfillment and ego identity can be provided through the partner, but (d) a number of difficulties could arise in the partnership. (e) Communications would be important but might be misunderstood by others and/or the public-at-large and create problems in the personality of the individual. (f) This negative impression might be averted by considering one's public image and/or being sensitive to others and taking action. (g) Another problem that could be manifested is that the charm and charisma which are evident in the partnership area might be stilted, (h) but this can be alleviated by again considering the public image, analyzing deeply and then taking action. _____

3. (a) Partnerships will be intensely emotional, and (b) the native or the partner may be possessive. (c) There is also, however, a desire to grow and develop with the partner, particularly philosophically. (d) The partner might be hard driving in the relationship on the one hand and yet (e) jovial and outgoing on the other. _____

EXERCISE 73   Chart Interpretation 7

Partnership (Seventh House)

A. Chart A—**House placement of ruler or co-rulers**: Moon (☽) in the eighth house

Major configurations and aspects to the ruler or co-rulers: Moon (☽), involved in a mutable T-Square, is conjunct Neptune (♆) and Mercury (☿) and square the Nodes (☊); it is also part of an earth Grand Trine with Jupiter (♃), Ascendant and Uranus (♅) and is quintile Venus (♀) and Mars (♂).

B. Chart B—**House placement of ruler or co-rulers**: Mars (♂) in the third house and Pluto (♇) in the fourth house

Major configurations and aspects to the ruler or co-rulers: Mars (♂) is conjunct Moon (☽) and Saturn (♄), opposition MC, trine Sun (☉) and square Mercury (☿); Pluto (♇) in a cradle, trines Mercury (☿), sextiles Uranus (♅) and Neptune (♆), and it semi-squares North Node (☊).

C. Chart C—**House placement of ruler or co-rulers**: Mars (♂) in the fifth house and Pluto (♇) in the fourth house

Major configurations and aspects to the ruler or co-rulers: Mars (♂) is conjunct Neptune (♆), sextile Sun (☉), Venus (♀), Jupiter (♃) and Part of Fortune (⊗), trine MC and sesqui-quadrate Uranus (♅); Pluto (♇) conjuncts South Node (☋) and Part of Fortune (⊗), opposes MC, Moon (☽) and North Node (☊), trines Sun (☉) and Venus (♀) and squares Mercury (☿) and Uranus (♅).

1. (a) There is a strong connection between communications and partnership. (b) A shared home is also essential, and the native wants to control the home area. (c) Communications could flow easily if ego needs are considered and (d) conversations are organized and (e) analyzed. (f) It is likely, however, that communications would be emotionally toned and (g) sometimes held back, and (h) profession might interfere. (i) The need for power could create problems if others influence the native to exert this power in partnerships. (j) There is, however, the ability to be sensitive to the needs of the partner and (k) to change suddenly. _____

2. (a) There is a strong connection between home and partnership—a compelling need for a partner with whom to share the home. (b) Romance or creativity is also a facet of the partnership. (c) The combining of initiative with charm, magnetism and charisma in dealing with the world and the

EXERCISE 73   Chart Interpretation 7

partner can be a definite asset but may be deceptive and sporadic. (d) There is also a desire for power in partnerships which would give the native a sense of fulfillment and provide pleasure for both the native and the partner. However, (e) others with whom he or she relates and communicates, or the public or world generally, might view the partnership as unusual or erratic. _____

3. (a) Sex or the partner's resources would be important in close one-to-one relationships and could provide both emotional and material security. (b) Other relationships might interfere with the partnership, but (c) when the native is sensitive to the needs of the partner and (d) takes the initiative in expressing affection in a creative, gentle way, (e) the rewards can be very great. _____

EXERCISE 74

Chart Interpretation 8

The Home (Fourth House)

Place the appropriate letter next to each description given below.

a. Chart A—**Signs in the 4th house**: Taurus (♉) and Gemini (♊)
Planets and points in the house: Uranus (♅)
Major configurations and aspects to the planets and points in the house: Uranus (♅) is part of an earth Grand Trine, including Ascendant, Jupiter (♃), Mercury (☿), Neptune (♆) and Moon (☽); it is also part of a fixed T-Square with MC, Part of Fortune (⊗) and Sun (☉) and is quincunx North Node (☊).

B. Chart B—**Signs in the 4th house**: Cancer (♋) and Leo (♌)
Planets and points in the house: Pluto (♀)
Major configurations and aspects to the planets and points in the house: Pluto (♀) trines Mercury (☿), sextiles Uranus (♅) and Neptune (♆) and semi-squares North Node (☊).

C. Chart C—**Signs in the 4th house**: Cancer (♋) and Leo (♌)
Planets and points in the house: South Node (☋) and Pluto (♀)

Major configurations and aspects to the planets and points in the house: South Node (☋) is part of a fixed Grand Cross, widely conjunct Pluto (♀), opposition North Node (☊) conjunct Moon (☽), square Ascendant on one side and Mercury (☿) conjunct Jupiter (♃) on the other, also square Uranus (♅); Pluto (♀) also opposes the North Node (☊)-Moon (☽) conjunction and the MC, trines the Sun (☉)-Venus (♀) conjunction, squares Mercury (☿) and Uranus (♅) and conjuncts the Part of Fortune (⊗).

1. (a) The home is a place where the individual can be motherly and protective, but where mothering and protection are needed as well. (b) It should also be warm and comfortable and an area in which the native can "shine" and be the center of attention. (c) The individual also wishes to be the power in the home which (d) can create problems in relationships. (e) Sensitivity to others and (f) discussion of problems can alleviate these problems (g) suddenly or in an unusual manner. _____

2. (a) The home area should be a place of emotional security which is also (b) warm and comfortable. The native enjoys being the center of attention and (c) definitely wants to be in control of the home situation. (d) The need for power can erupt suddenly but may be easily masked in the home with charm. (e) Relating to others in the home is essential but will

EXERCISE 74 Chart Interpretation 8

be very complex and may be difficult. (f) In relationships the emotions and consideration of the public image must be balanced with the need for power to achieve self-fulfillment. (g) The individual must be wary of making grand promises which would reflect negatively on the personality generally.

3. (a) The individual obtains material security through the home and likes to be surrounded by beauty there. (b) It is also a place to communicate and socialize with others. (c) It may be an unusual place or an area where the individual wants freedom and independence. (d) The need for ego gratification and self-fulfillment through others might interfere with the independence and (e) cause the individual to end relationships abruptly. (f) For the most part, however, energies should flow easily in the home, especially if the native is (g) materially secure and (h) expresses his or her own personality and (i) emotions freely. (j) Then home can be a sanctuary.

EXERCISE 75　　　　　Chart Interpretation 9

The Home (Fourth House)

A. Chart A—**House placement of ruler or co-rulers**: Venus (♀) in the sixth house
Major configurations and aspects to the ruler or co-rulers:
Venus (♀) is square Saturn (♄), quintile Moon (☽) and Neptune (♆), bi-quintile Mars (♂), sextile Mercury (☿), trine MC and sesqui-quadrate Part of Fortune (⊗).

B. Chart B—**House placement of ruler or co-rulers**: Moon (☽) in the third house
Major configurations and aspects to the ruler or co-rulers:
Moon (☽), part of a cardinal T-Square, is conjunct Saturn (♄), opposition MC and square Jupiter (♃); it also trines Sun (☉) and conjuncts Mars (♂).

C. Chart C—**House placement of the ruler or co-rulers**: Moon (☽) in the tenth house
Major configurations and aspects to the ruler or co-rulers:
Moon (☽), part of a fixed Grand Cross, is conjunct North Node (☊), opposition South Node (☋), and square Ascendant on one side, and Jupiter (♃) conjunct Mercury (☿) on the other; it also squares Uranus (♅) and opposes Pluto (♇).

1. (a) Order and routine are emphasized in the home. (b) austerity or too much structure might sometimes interfere with the pleasure of the home, but (c) usually most of the needs should be easily satisfied. (d) Artistic ability and (e) the emotions (f) can be expressed in that area without much effort. (g) It is also a place where action regarding other areas, even the career, may be begun. (h) Such action may result in self-fulfillment. _____

2. (a) The individual will relate to the world from the home base or will bring career into the home, but (b) this area will be complex and will present difficulties. (c) As stated previously, the native must relate and communicate with others in the home, and (d) the personality plays an essential role. (e) He or she should, however, be careful in emotional discussions not to make grand promises that cannot be kept because (f) such behavior would cause others to react negatively to the individual. (g) This reaction could occur suddenly and powerfully. _____

3. (a) Communications are important in the home area. (b) They

EXERCISE 75   Chart Interpretation 9

may be emotionally colored. (c) They will at times be energetic and (d) at times restrained, and (e) emotional outbursts will occur especially if (f) there are tensions from the career. (g) The individual, however can easily "shine" in the home if ego needs are being expressed and satisfied.

_____

Martin Luther King
January 15, 1929
1200 Hrs. C.S.T.
Atlanta, Georgia

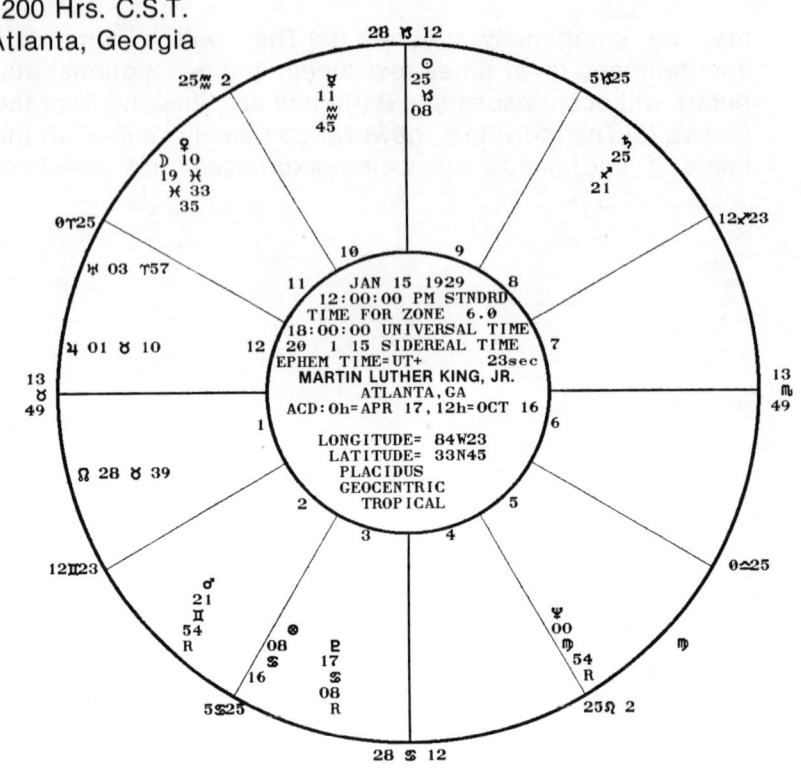

| Sun | ♑ | Moon | ♓ | Ascendant | ♉ |

Stelliums _____

		by Sign	by House
Elements:	Fire	♅ ♄	♆ ☉
	Earth	♃ A ♆ ☉ MC	♂ ☿
	Air	♂ ☿	♀ ♀ ☽
	Water	♀ ♀ ☽	♄ ♅ ♃
Modes:	Cardinal	♅ ♇ ☉ MC	☿
	Fixed	♃ ☿ A	♂ ♆ ♄ ♀ ☽
	Mutable	♂ ♆ ♄ ♀ ☽	♀ ☉ ♅ ♃
Sign Emphasis:		♍	♒ ♏

Martin Luther King

Major Configurations:

earth-fire (♄ ♃ ♆ triangle)

mutable T-square: ☽ — ♂ — ♄

fixed-mutable T-square: ☊ — ♇ — ⯝

	☉										
☽	✱	☽									
☿			☿								
♀	∠		⚹	♀							
♂		□		♂							
♃	□				♃						
♄	⚹	□	∠	☍	△	♄					
♅			✱				♅				
♆	±			△	△		♆				
♇	☍	△		△			∠	♇			
A		✱	□	✱				✱	A		
M	☌			±	□	✱			M		
☊	△				✱	□		△	☊		
⊗			△	✱		□	✱	✱			

The most heavily emphasized signs are Capricorn (☉), Pisces (Moon), Taurus (Ascendant), Virgo (emphasis by sign), Aquarius (emphasis by house) and Scorpio (emphasis by house).

The major configurations are a Grand Trine in earth-fire (Jupiter trine Neptune, trine Saturn), a mutable T-Square (Mars opposition Saturn, square Moon) and a fixed-mutable T-Square (Node axis square Neptune).

EXERCISE 76

Martin Luther King

Martin Luther King

Write a paragraph describing King according to the signs emphasized in his chart.

Capricorn (♑), Pisces (♓) and Taurus (♉); followed by Virgo (♍), Aquarius (♒) and Scorpio (♏). (When no sign is emphasized more than once, begin with the signs of the Sun (☉), Moon (☽) and Ascendant.)

EXERCISE 77　　　　　King's Configurations

Martin Luther King
Major Configurations

Give a short description of a possible manifestation of each of the major configurations which appear in Martin Luther King's chart.

1. Grand Trine in earth-fire: Saturn (♄) trine Neptune (♆), trine Jupiter (♃).
2. Mutable T-Square: Mars (♂) opposition Saturn (♄), square Moon (☽).
3. Fixed-mutable T-Square: The Node axis (☊☋) square Neptune (♆).

EXERCISE 78   King's Career 1

Martin Luther King
Career (Tenth House)

As in exercises 70-75, there is a division into two parts. Write short paragraphs to describe the requirements of each area, according to the signs, planets, points and aspects given below.

Signs in the 10th house: Capricorn (♑) and Aquarius (♒)

Planets and points in the house: Mercury (☿)

Major configurations and aspects to the planets and points in the house: Mercury (☿) is semi-sextile Venus (♀), semi-square Saturn (♄), sextile Uranus (♅) and square Ascendant.

EXERCISE 79   King's Career 2

Martin Luther King
Career (Tenth House)

House placement of ruler or co-rulers: Saturn (♄) in the eighth house

Major configurations and aspects to the ruler or co-rulers: Saturn (♄), part of a Grand Trine in earth-fire, is trine Jupiter (♃) and Neptune (♆); it is also part of a mutable T-Square with Mars (♂) and Moon (☽); and is semi-sextile Sun (☉) and semi-square Mercury (☿).

EXERCISE 80   King's Partnerships 1

Martin Luther King
Partnership (Seventh House)

Signs in the 7th house: Scorpio (♏) and Sagittarius (♐)

Planets and points in the house: South Node (☋)

Major configurations and aspects to the planets and points in the house: South Node (☋), in a fixed-mutable T-Square, squares Neptune (♆) and opposes North Node (☊); it also sextiles Sun (☉) and MC and trines Uranus (♅).

EXERCISE 81   King's Partnerships 2

Martin Luther King:
Partnership (Seventh House)

House placement of ruler or co-rulers: Mars (♂) in the second house and Pluto (♇) in the third house

Major configurations and aspects to the ruler or co-rulers: Mars (♂), part of a mutable T-Square, is opposition Saturn (♄) and square Moon (☽), and it is also bi-quintile MC; Pluto (♇) opposes Sun (☉), semi-squares Neptune (♆), sextiles Ascendant and trines Moon (☽) and Venus (♀).

EXERCISE 82 — King's Communications 1

Martin Luther King
Communications (Third House)

Signs in the 3rd house: Cancer (♋)

Planets and points in the house: Part of Fortune (⊗) and Pluto (♇)

Major configurations and aspects to the planets and points in the house: Part of Fortune (⊗) trines Venus (♀), squares Uranus (♅), sextiles Jupiter (♃), Neptune (♆) and Ascendant; Pluto (♇) opposes Sun (☉), trines Moon (☽) and Venus (♀), semi-squares Neptune (♆) and sextiles Ascendant.

EXERCISE 83 — King's Communications 2

Martin Luther King
Communications (Third House)

House placement of ruler or co-rulers: Moon (☽) in the eleventh house

Major configurations and aspects to the ruler or co-rulers: Moon (☽), part of a mutable T-Square, is square Mars (♂) on the one side and Saturn (♄) on the other; it also trines Pluto (♇) and sextiles Ascendant and Sun (☉).

Eleanor Roosevelt
October 11, 1884
11:00 Hrs. E.S.T.
New York, N.Y.

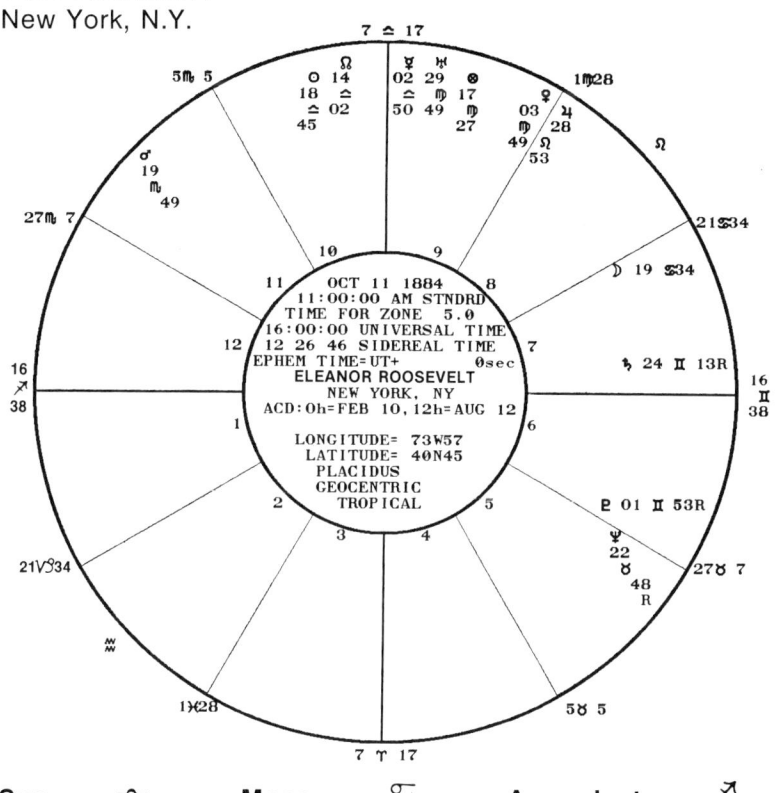

		by Sign	by House
Elements:	Fire	♃ A	♇ ♀ ♅ ☿
	Earth	♇ ♀ ♅	♀ ☉
	Air	♀ ♄ ☿ MC ☉	♄ ☽ ♂
	Water	☽ ♂	♃
Modes:	Cardinal	☽ ☿ MC ☉	♄ ☽ ☉
	Fixed	♇ ♃ ♂	♇ ♃ ♂
	Mutable	♀ ♄ ♀ ♅ A	♀ ♀ ♅ ☿
Sign Emphasis:		♊	♐

Sun ♎ Moon ♋ Ascendant ♐
Stelliums 9th house

Eleanor Roosevelt **Major Configurations:**

The most heavily emphasized sign is Sagittarius (Ascendant, ninth house stellium and emphasis by house). Libra (Sun), Cancer (Moon) and Gemini (emphasis by sign) follow in importance and should be incorporated into an overall synthesis after the first sign is interpreted.

The major configurations are a fixed T-Square (Mars opposition Neptune, square Jupiter*), a mutable T-Square (Ascendant opposition Saturn, square Part of Fortune), a cardinal T-Square (Sun conjunct North Node, opposition South Node, square Moon) and a Cradle (Mars sextile Part of Fortune, sextile Moon, sextile Neptune).

*I sometimes extend the orb when one planet in a major configuration aspects two planets which are slightly out of orb.

EXERCISE 84   Eleanor Roosevelt

Eleanor Roosevelt

Write a paragraph describing Eleanor Roosevelt according to the signs emphasized in her chart.

Sagittarius (♐); followed by Libra (♎), Cancer (♋) and Gemini (♊).

EXERCISE 85 — Roosevelt's Configurations

Eleanor Roosevelt
Major Configurations

Give a short description of possible manifestations of each of the major configurations which appear in Eleanor Roosevelt's chart.

1. Fixed T-Square: Mars (♂) opposition Neptune (♆), square Jupiter (♃).

2. Mutable T-Square: Ascendant opposition Saturn (♄), square Part of Fortune (⊗).

3. Cradle: Mars (♂) sextile Part of Fortune (⊗), sextile Moon (☽), sextile Neptune (♆).

4. Cardinal T-Square: Sun (☉) conjunct North Node (☊), opposition South Node (☋), square Moon (☽).

EXERCISE 86 Roosevelt's Distant Travel 1

Eleanor Roosevelt
Distant Travel (Ninth House)

Write short paragraphs to describe the requirements of each area, according to the signs, planets, points and aspects given below.

Signs in the 9th house: Virgo (♍) and Libra (♎)

Planets and points in the house: Venus (♀), Part of Fortune (⊗), Uranus (♅) and Mercury (☿)

Major configurations and aspects to the planets and points in the house: Venus (♀) is conjunct Jupiter (♃), square Pluto (♇), semi-square Sun (☉) and Moon (☽) and semi-sextile Mercury (☿); Part of Fortune (⊗) is part of a mutable T-Square: square Ascendant and Saturn (♄); and part of a Cradle: sextile Mars (♂) and Moon (☽) and trine Neptune (♆); it is also semi-sextile Sun (☉); Uranus (♅) and Mercury (☿) are conjunct, and they both quintile Moon (☽), square Saturn (♄),* trine Pluto (♇) and conjunct MC; Mercury (☿) also semi-sextiles Venus (♀), semi-squares Mars (♂) and quintiles Ascendant; Uranus (♅) is also semi-sextile Jupiter (♃) and trine Neptune (♆).

* Mercury is pulled into orb of a square to Saturn by its conjunction to Uranus.

EXERCISE 87 Roosevelt's Distant Travel 2

Eleanor Roosevelt
Distant Travel (ninth house)

House placement of ruler or co-rulers: Mercury (☿) in the ninth house

Major configurations and aspects to the ruler or co-rulers: Mercury (☿) aspects are given in Exercise 86.

EXERCISE 88   Roosevelt's Publishing 1

Eleanor Roosevelt
Publishing (Ninth House)

Signs in the 9th house: Virgo (♍) and Libra (♎)

Planets and points in the house: Venus (♀), Part of Fortune (⊗), Uranus (♅) and Mercury (☿)

Major configurations and aspects to the planets and points in the house: Venus (♀) is conjunct Jupiter (♃), square Pluto (♇), semi-square Sun (☉) and Moon (☽) and semi-sextile Mercury (☿); Part of Fortune (⊗) is part of a mutable T-Square: square Ascendant and Saturn (♄); and part of a Cradle: sextile Mars (♂) and Moon (☽) and trine Neptune (♆); it is also semi-sextile Sun (☉); Uranus (♅) and Mercury (☿) are conjunct, and they both quintile Moon (☽), square Saturn (♄), trine Pluto (♇) and conjunct MC; Mercury (☿) also semi-sextiles Venus (♀) semi-squares Mars (♂) and quintiles Ascendant; Uranus (♅) is also semi-sextile Jupiter (♃) and trine Neptune (♆).

EXERCISE 89   Roosevelt's Publishing 2

Eleanor Roosevelt
Publishing (Ninth House)

House placement of ruler or co-rulers: Mercury (☿) in the ninth house

Major configurations and aspects to the ruler or co-rulers: Mercury (☿) aspects are given in Exercise 88.

EXERCISE 90 — Roosevelt's Partnerships 1

Eleanor Roosevelt
Partnership (Seventh House)

Signs in the 7th house: Gemini (♊) and Cancer (♋)

Planets and points in the house: Saturn (♄) and Moon (☽)

Major configurations and aspects to the planets and points in the house: Saturn (♄), part of a mutable T-Square, is opposition Ascendant and square Part of Fortune (⊗); it is also trine Sun (☉), bi-quintile Mars (♂), sextile Jupiter (♃), square Mercury (☿) conjunct Uranus (♅), and semi-sextile Neptune (♆); Moon (☽), part of a Cradle, is sextile Part of Fortune (⊗) and Neptune (♆) and trine Mars (♂); part of a cardinal T-Square, it is square North Node (☊) and Sun (☉) on one side and South Node (☋) on the other; it also quintiles Mercury (☿) and Uranus (♅) and semi-squares Venus (♀).

EXERCISE 91 — Roosevelt's Partnerships 2

Eleanor Roosevelt
Partnership (Seventh House)

House placement of ruler or co-rulers: Mercury (☿) in the ninth house

Major configurations and aspects to the ruler or co-rulers: Mercury (☿) is quintile Moon (☽) and Ascendant, semi-sextile Venus (♀), semi-square Mars (♂), square Saturn (♄), conjunct Uranus (♅) and MC, and trine Pluto (♇).

Babe Ruth
February 6, 1895
13:45 Hrs. E.S.T.
Baltimore, Md.

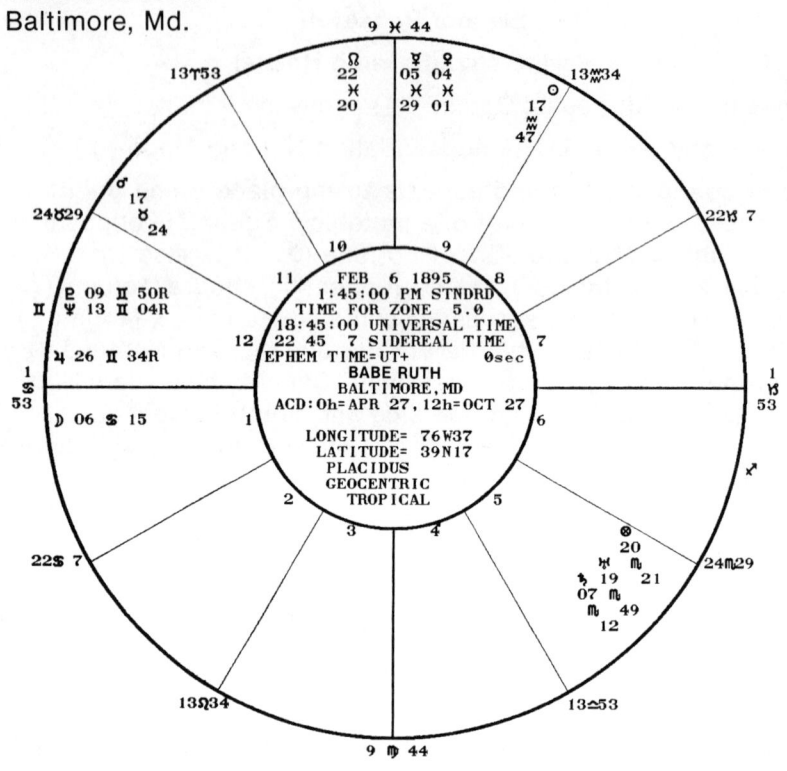

		by Sign	by House
Elements:	Fire		☽ ♄ ♅ ☉ ♀ ☿
	Earth	♂	
	Air	☿ ♆ ♃ ☉	♂
	Water	A ☽ ♄ ♅ ♀ ☿ MC	♀ ♆ ♃
Modes:	Cardinal	☽ A	☽
	Fixed	♂ ♄ ♅ ☉	♄ ♅ ♂
	Mutable	♀ ♆ ♃ ☿ ♀ MC	☉ ♀ ☿ ♀ ♆ ♃
Sign Emphasis:		♓	♐

Sun ♒   Moon ♋   Ascendant ♋
Stelliums ♊, 9th house-12th house

112

Babe Ruth

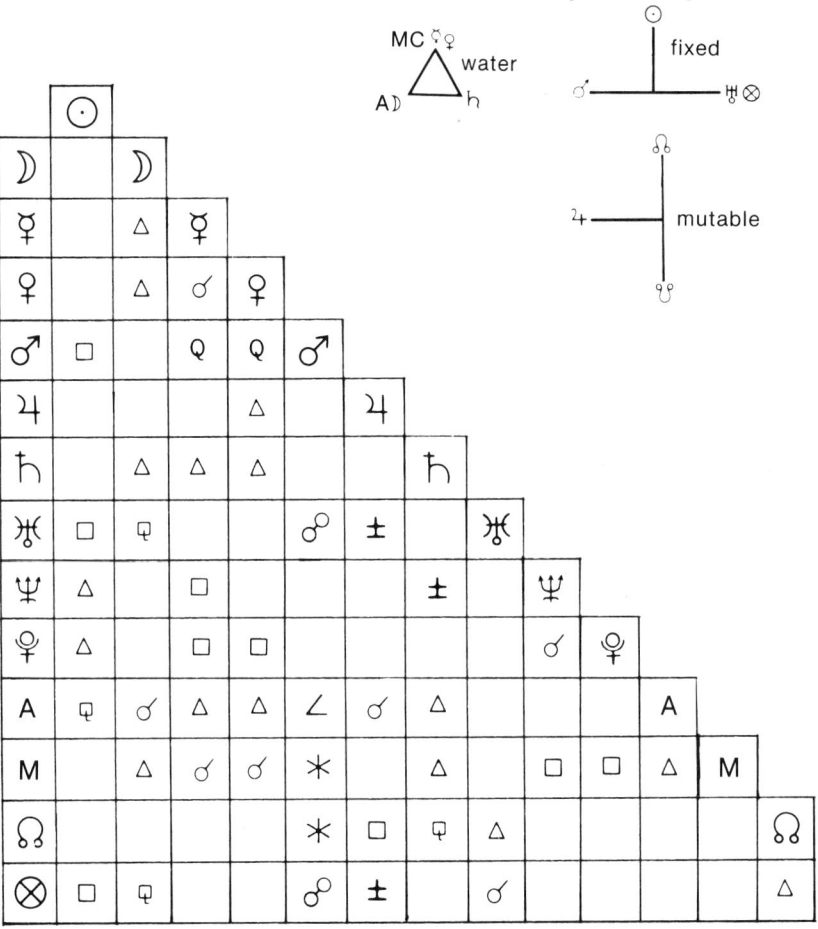

The most heavily emphasized signs are Cancer (Moon and Ascendant), Pisces (twelfth house stellium and emphasis by sign) and Sagittarius (ninth house stellium and emphasis by house). Aquarius (Sun) and Gemini (stellium) follow in importance and should be incorporated into an overall synthesis after the first three signs are integrated.

The major configurations are a Grand Trine in water (Ascendant conjunct Moon, trine Saturn, trine Venus conjunct Mercury and MC); a fixed T-Square (Mars opposition Uranus conjunct Part of Fortune, square Sun); and a mutable T-Square (Jupiter square the Node axis).

EXERCISE 92 Babe Ruth

Babe Ruth

Write a paragraph describing Babe Ruth according to the signs emphasized in his chart.

Cancer (♋), Pisces (♓) and Sagittarius (♐); followed by Aquarius (♒) and Gemini (♊).

EXERCISE 93 — Ruth's Configurations

Babe Ruth
Major Configurations

Give a short description of possible manifestations of each of the major configurations which appear in Babe Ruth's chart.

1. Fixed T-Square: Mars (♂) opposition Uranus (♅) conjunct Part of Fortune (⊗) square Sun (☉).

2. Grand Trine in water: Ascendant conjunct Moon (☽), trine Saturn (♄), trine Venus (♀) conjunct Mercury (☿) and MC.

3. Mutable T-Square: The Node axis (☊☋) square Jupiter (♃).

EXERCISE 94   Ruth's Athletics 1

Babe Ruth
Athletics (Ninth House)

As previously stated, each house has a number of possible meanings. Since babe Ruth was a talented athlete, we are examining the ninth house from that point of view.

Signs in the 9th house: Aquarius (♒) and Pisces (♓)

Planets and points in the house: Sun (☉), Venus (♀) and Mercury (☿)

Major configurations and aspects to the planets and points in the house: Sun (☉), part of a fixed T-Square, is square Mars (♂) on one side and Uranus (♅) conjunct Part of Fortune (⊗) on the other; it is also trine Neptune (♆) and Pluto (♇) and sesqui-quadrate Ascendant; Venus (♀) and Mercury (☿) are conjunct and part of a Grand Trine in water, conjunct MC, trine Saturn (♄) and trine Ascendant conjunct Moon (☽); they are also quintile Mars (♂) and square Pluto (♇); Mercury (☿) is square Neptune (♆) as well; and Venus (♀) is trine Jupiter (♃).

EXERCISE 95   Ruth's Athletics 2

Babe Ruth
Athletics (Ninth House)

House placement of ruler or co-rulers: Saturn (♄) and Uranus (♅), both in the fifth house

Major configurations and aspects to the ruler or co-rulers: Saturn (♄), part of a Grand Trine in water, is trine Venus (♀) conjunct Mercury (☿) and MC and trine Ascendant conjunct Moon (☽); Saturn is also sesqui-quadrate North Node (☊) and bi-quintile Neptune (♆); Uranus (♅), part of a fixed T-Square, is conjunct Part of Fortune (⊗), opposition Mars (♂) and square Sun (☉); it is also sesqui-quadrate Moon (☽), bi-quintile Jupiter (♃) and trine North Node (☊).

EXERCISE 96　　　Ruth's Group Involvement 1

Group Involvement (Eleventh House)

Since Babe Ruth was a member of a baseball team we will examine his group involvement, which is an eleventh house matter.

Signs in the 11th house: Aries (♈) and Taurus (♉)
Planets and points in the house: Mars (♂)

Major configurations and aspects to the planets and points in the house: Mars (♂), part of a fixed T-Square, is opposition Uranus (♅) conjunct the Part of Fortune (⊗), square Sun (☉); it is also quintile Mercury (☿) and Venus (♀), sextile MC and North Node (☊) and semi-square Ascendant.

EXERCISE 97　　　Ruth's Group Involvement 2
Babe Ruth
Group Involvement (Eleventh House)

House placement of ruler or co-rulers: Mars (♂) in the eleventh house

Major Configurations and aspects to the ruler or co-rulers: Mars (♂) aspects are given in Exercise 96.

EXERCISE 98 — Ruth's Partnerships 1

Babe Ruth
Partnership (Seventh House)

Now that we have investigated Babe Ruth's group activities, let us see how his partnerships or close one-to-one relationships were similar to or different from his group involvement.

Signs in the 7th house: Capricorn (♑)

Planets and points in the house: None

Major configurations and aspects to the planets and points in the house: None

EXERCISE 99 — Ruth's Partnerships 2

Babe Ruth
Partnership (Seventh House)

House placement of ruler or co-rulers: Saturn (♄) in the fifth house

Major configurations and aspects to the ruler or co-rulers: Saturn (♄), part of a Grand Trine in water, is trine Venus (♀) conjunct Mercury (☿) and MC, and trine Ascendant conjunct Moon (☽); it is also sesqui-quadrate North Node (☊) and bi-quintile Neptune (♆).

ANSWERS

EXERCISE 1
1. h. Positive signs (+) ♈ ♊ ♌ ♎ ♐ ♒
2. d. Water signs ♋ ♏ ♓
3. e. Cardinal signs ♈ ♋ ♎ ♑
4. b. Earth signs ♉ ♍ ♑
5. c. Air signs ♊ ♎ ♒
6. i. Negative signs (-) ♉ ♋ ♍ ♏ ♑ ♓
7. g. Mutable signs ♊ ♍ ♐ ♓
8. a. Fire signs ♈ ♌ ♐
9. f. Fixed signs ♉ ♌ ♏ ♒

EXERCISE 2
I.   a. 3. Gemini ♊   g. 2. Taurus ♉
    b. 1. Aries ♈   h. 10. Capricorn ♑
    c. 12. Pisces ♓   i. 4. Cancer ♋
    d. 7. Libra ♎   j. 11. Aquarius ♒
    e. 6. Virgo ♍   k. 5. Leo ♌
    f. 9. Sagittarius ♐ l. 8. Scorpio ♏
II. a. 3. Gemini ♊; and 6. Virgo ♍
    b. 12. Pisces ♓
    c. 4. Cancer ♋
    d. 1. Aries ♈
    e. 8. Scorpio ♏
    f. 11. Aquarius ♒
    g. 2. Taurus ♉; and 7. Libra ♎
    h. 5. Leo ♌
    i. 10. Capricorn ♑
    j. 9. Sagittarius ♐

EXERCISE 3
1. a. Cancer ♋
2. b. Gemini ♊;   d. Leo ♌;
   f. Libra ♎;   h. Sagittarius ♐;
   j. Aquarius ♒
3. i. Capricorn ♑;   (a. Taurus ♉)*
4. k. Pisces ♓;   e. Virgo ♍;
   a. Taurus ♉
5. d. Leo ♌;   h. Sagittarius ♐
6. b. Gemini ♊;   (f. Libra ♎;
   j. Aquarius ♒;   h. Sagittarius ♐)
7. e. Virgo ♍;   (a. Taurus ♉;
   g. Scorpio ♏;   i. Capricorn ♑)
8. c. Cancer ♋;   f. Libra ♎;
   j. Aquarius ♒
9. i. Capricorn ♑
10. k. Pisces ♓;   (c. Cancer   )

* The signs of secondary importance for modification have been placed in parentheses.

EXERCISE 4
1. g. Scorpio ♏;   i. Capricorn ♑;
   (d. Leo ♌;   j. Aquarius ♒)
2. b. Gemini ♊;   e. Virgo ♍;
   h. Sagittarius ♐;   k. Pisces ♓;
   (f. Libra ♎)
3. e. Virgo ♍;   i. Capricorn ♑
4. c. Cancer ♋
5. f. Libra ♎
6. g. Scorpio ♏
7. c. Cancer ♋;   g. Scorpio ♏;
   k. Pisces ♓
8. d. Leo ♌
9. a. Aries ♈;   d. Leo ♌ ;
   h. Sagittarius ♐
10. b. Gemini ♊;   (h. Sagittarius ♐)

EXERCISE 5
1. b. Taurus ♉;   d. Leo ♌; g. Scorpio ♏;
   (i. Capricorn ♑)   j. Aquarius ♒;
2. e. Virgo ♍;   h. Sagittarius ♐;
   k. Pisces ♓;   (f. Libra ♎)
3. j. Aquarius ♒
4. h. Sagittarius ♐
5. a. Aries ♈;   d. Leo ♌;
   h. Sagittarius ♐
6. b. Taurus ♉;   e. Virgo ♍;
   i. Capricorn ♑
7. c. Cancer ♋;   g. Scorpio ♏;
   k. Pisces ♓
8. f. Libra ♎
9. e. Virgo ♍;   g. Scorpio ♏
10. a. Aries ♈

EXERCISE 6
1. b. Taurus ♉;   e. Virgo ♍;
   i. Capricorn ♑
2. g. Scorpio ♏;   k. Pisces ♓
3. h. Sagittarius ♐
4. c. Gemini ♊;   (f. Libra ♎;
   j. Aquarius ♒)
5. a. Aries ♈
6. a. Aries ♈;   d. Leo ♌;
   h. Sagittarius ♐
7. e. Virgo ♍
8. f. Libra ♎
9. a. Aries ♈;   c. Gemini ♊;
   d. Leo ♌;   f. Libra ♎;
   h. Sagittarius ♐;   j. Aquarius ♒
10. j. Aquarius ♒

EXERCISE 7
1. b. Taurus ♉; e. Virgo ♍;
   i. Capricorn ♑
2. k. Pisces ♓
3. c. Gemini ♊; e. Virgo ♍;
   h. Sagittarius ♐; k. Pisces ♓
4. a. Aries ♈; h. Sagittarius ♐
5. f. Libra ♎; j. Aquarius ♒
6. b. Taurus ♉; g. Scorpio ♏;
   j. Aquarius ♒; (i. Capricorn ♑)
7. d. Cancer ♋
8. f. Libra ♎
9. d. Cancer ♋; g. Scorpio ♏;
   k. Pisces ♓
10. b. Taurus ♉; d. Cancer ♋;
    e. Virgo ♍; g. Scorpio ♏;
    i. Capricorn ♑; k. Pisces ♓

EXERCISE 8
1. k. Pisces ♓
2. b. Taurus ♉; i. Capricorn ♑
3. c. Gemini ♊
4. h. Sagittarius ♐
5. a. Aries ♈; e. Leo ♌;
   h. Sagittarius ♐
6. g. Scorpio ♏
7. f. Libra ♎
8. j. Aquarius ♒
9. d. Cancer ♋
10. b. Taurus ♉; e. Leo ♌;
    g. Scorpio ♏; j. Aquarius ♒;
    (i. Capricorn ♑)

EXERCISE 9

1. a. Aries ♈
2. h. Sagittarius ♐
3. i. Capricorn ♑
4. d. Cancer ♋
5. b. Taurus ♉
6. a. Aries ♈ ;   e. Leo ♌ ;
   h. Sagittarius ♐
7. b. Taurus ♉ ;   f. Virgo ♍ ;
   i. Capricorn ♑
8. d. Cancer ♋ ;   g. Scorpio ♏ ;
   k. Pisces ♓
9. j. Aquarius ♒
10. c. Gemini ♊

EXERCISE 10

1. i. Capricorn ♑
2. a. Aries ♈ ;   c. Gemini ♊ ;
   e. Leo ♌ ;   g. Libra ♎ ;
   h. Sagittarius ♐ ; j. Aquarius ♒
3. f. Virgo ♍
4. h. Sagittarius ♐
5. d. Cancer ♋
6. d. Cancer ♋ ;   k. Pisces ♓
7. b. Taurus ♉ ;   f. Virgo ♍ ;
   i. Capricorn ♑
8. h. Sagittarius ♐
9. c. Gemini ♊ ;   g. Libra ♎ ;
   j. Aquarius ♒
10. g. Libra ♎

EXERCISE 11
1. d. Cancer ♋
2. k. Pisces ♓
3. a. Aries ♈ ;   e. Leo ♌
4. j. Aquarius ♒
5. b. Taurus ♉ ;   d. Cancer ♋ ;
   f. Virgo ♍ ;   h. Scorpio ♏ ;
   i. Capricorn ♑ ;   k. Pisces ♓
6. c. Gemini— ♊
7. g. Libra— ♎
8. b. Taurus— ♉ ;   f. Virgo—♍;
   i. Capricorn—♑
9. f. Virgo— ♍   k. Pisces—♓
10. h. Scorpio—♏;   i. Capricorn—♑;
    (b.Taurus— ♉ ;   d. Cancer —♋;
    f. Virgo—♍;   k. Pisces—♓)

EXERCISE 12
1. k. Pisces—♓
2. j. Aquarius—♒
3. g. Libra—♎
4. b. Taurus— ♉ ;   h. Scorpio— ♏
   (e.Leo—♌;   j. Aquarius—♒)
5. a. Aries— ♈ ;   (c.Gemini—♊)
6. c. Gemini— ♊
7. a. Aries—♈ ;   c. Gemini— ♊ ;
   e. Leo—♌;   g. Libra—♎;
   i. Sagittarius— ♐;   j. Aquarius— ♒
8. d. Cancer— ♋   h. Scorpio—♏;
   k. Pisces— ♓
9. e. Leo—♌
10. i. Sagittarius— ♐

EXERCISE 13
1. d. Cancer—♋;   h. Scorpio—♏;
   k. Pisces—♓
2. c. Gemini—♊;   g. Libra—♎;
   (f. Virgo—♍;   i. Sagittarius—♐)
3. j. Capricorn—♑   (b. Taurus—♉;
   f. Virgo—♍;   h. Scorpio—♏)
4. a. Aries—♈
5. i. Sagittarius—♐
6. e. Leo—♌
7. b. Taurus—♉;
   f. Virgo—♍;   j. Capricorn—♑
8. g. Libra—♎
9. a. Aries—♈;   e. Leo—♌;
   i. Sagittarius—♐
10. d. Cancer—♋

EXERCISE 14
1. d. Cancer—♋;   h. Scorpio—♏
2. b. Taurus—♉;   f. Virgo—♍;
   j. Capricorn—♑;
3. i. Sagittarius—♐
4. a. Aries—♈
5. g. Libra—♎
6. k. Aquarius—♒
7. a. Aries—♈;   e. Leo♌;
   i. Sagittarius—♐
8. c. Gemini—♊;   g. Libra—♎;
   k. Aquarius—♒;   (f. Virgo—♍)
9. c. Gemini—♊;   f. Virgo—♍;
   i. Sagittarius—♐
10. e. Leo—♌

EXERCISE 15
1. f. Leo—♌; Aquarius—♒; Pisces—♓
2. a. Aries—♈; Cancer—♋; Capricorn—♑
3. g. Taurus—♉; Gemini—♊; Sagittarius—♐
4. h. Cancer—♋; Libra—♎; Scorpio—♏
5. c. Leo—♌; Virgo—♍; Libra—♎
6. b. Aries—♈; Scorpio—♏; Sagittarius—♐
7. d. Gemini—♊; Capricorn—♑; Aquarius—♒
8. e. Taurus—♉; Virgo—♍; Pisces—♓

EXERCISE 16
1. d. Taurus—♉; Cancer—♋; Virgo—♍
2. g. Scorpio—♏; Capricorn—♑; Pisces—♓
3. a. Aries—♈; Gemini—♊; Leo—♌
4. h. Taurus—♉; Capricorn—♑; Pisces—♓
5. c. Libra—♎; Sagittarius—♐; Aquarius—♒
6. e. Cancer—♋; Virgo—♍; Scorpio—♏
7. b. Leo—♌; Libra—♎; Sagittarius—♐
8. f. Virgo—♍; Scorpio—♏; Capricorn—♑

EXERCISE 17
1. d. Cancer—♋; Libra—♎; Capricorn—♑
2. f. Leo—♌; Scorpio—♏; Aquarius—♒
3. b. Taurus—♉; Gemini—♊; Cancer—♋
4. h. Aries—♈; Aquarius—♒; Pisces—♓
5. g. Gemini—♊; Virgo—♍; Aquarius—♒
6. c. Aries—♈; Leo—♌; Sagittarius—♐
7. a. Aries—♈; Sagittarius—♐; Aquarius—♒
8. e. Gemini—♊; Leo—♌; Libra—♎

EXERCISE 18
1. c. Virgo—♍; Sagittarius—♐; Pisces—♓
2. b. Cancer—♋; Scorpio—♏; Pisces—♓
3. d. Cancer—♋; Leo—♌; Sagittarius—♐
4. h. Scorpio—♏; Aquarius—♒; Pisces—♓
5. g. Gemini—♊; Virgo—♍; Scorpio—♏
6. f. Taurus—♉; Cancer—♋; Capricorn—♑
7. a. Aries—♈; Taurus—♉; Gemini—♊
8. e. Sagittarius—♐; Capricorn—♑; Aquarius—♒

EXERCISE 19
1. d. Aries— ♈; Sagittarius— ♐; Capricorn— ♑
2. c. Aries— ♈; Gemini— ♊; Cancer— ♋
3. f. Cancer— ♋; Libra— ♎; Pisces— ♓
4. h. Cancer— ♋; Leo— ♌; Virgo— ♍
5. a. Gemini— ♊; Cancer— ♋; Leo— ♌
6. b. Taurus— ♉; Virgo— ♍; Capricorn— ♑
7. g. Taurus— ♉; Leo— ♌; Scorpio— ♏
8. e. Gemini— ♊; Virgo— ♍; Sagittarius— ♐

EXERCISE 20
1. f. Aries— ♈; Taurus— ♉; Cancer— ♋
2. e. Leo— ♌; Virgo— ♍; Pisces— ♓
3. h. Libra— ♎; Sagittarius— ♐; Aquarius— ♒
4. b. Capricorn— ♑; Aquarius— ♒; Pisces— ♓
5. g. Cancer— ♋; Leo— ♌; Capricorn— ♑
6. d. Libra— ♎; Scorpio— ♏; Sagittarius— ♐
7. c. Gemini— ♊; Virgo— ♍; Pisces— ♓
8. a. Aries— ♈; Cancer— ♋; Libra— ♎

EXERCISE 21
1. a. Virgo— ♍; Libra— ♎; Scorpio— ♏
2. e. Scorpio— ♏; Sagittarius— ♐; Capricorn— ♑
3. b. Gemini— ♊; Sagittarius— ♐; Pisces— ♓
4. g. Taurus— ♉; Leo— ♌; Aquarius— ♒
5. c. Cancer— ♋; Sagittarius— ♐; Aquarius— ♒
6. h. Taurus— ♉; Virgo— ♍; Libra— ♎
7. f. Gemini— ♊; Libra— ♎; Aquarius— ♒
8. d. Aries— ♈; Leo— ♌; Capricorn— ♑

EXERCISE 22
1. b. Cancer— ♋; Virgo— ♍; Capricorn— ♑
2. c. Libra— ♎; Scorpio— ♏; Aquarius— ♒
3. a. Gemini— ♊; Leo— ♌; Sagittarius— ♐
4. g. Virgo— ♍; Scorpio— ♏; Sagittarius— ♐
5. f. Taurus— ♉; Gemini— ♊; Pisces— ♓
6. e. Aries— ♈; Libra— ♎; Capricorn— ♑
7. h. Cancer— ♋; Leo— ♌; Aquarius— ♒
8. d. Aries— ♈; Gemini— ♊; Pisces— ♓

EXERCISE 23
1. f. Virgo—♍; Libra—♎; Aquarius—♒
2. h. Gemini—♊; Aquarius—♒; Pisces—♓
3. d. Libra—♎; Scorpio—♏; Pisces—♓
4. e. Gemini—♊; Cancer—♋; Scorpio—♏
5. c. Leo—♌; Virgo—♍; Capricorn—♑
6. g. Aries—♈; Libra—♎; Sagittarius—♐
7. a. Taurus—♉; Scorpio—♏; Aquarius—♒
8. b. Cancer—♋; Leo—♌; Libra—♎

EXERCISE 24
1. e. Taurus—♉; Virgo—♍; Aquarius—♒
2. c. Cancer—♋; Scorpio—♏; Capricorn—♑
3. f. Aries—♈; Sagittarius—♐; Pisces—♓
4. a. Gemini—♊; Cancer—♋; Pisces—♓
5. h. Aries—♈; Taurus—♉; Scorpio—♏
6. b. Leo—♌; Scorpio—♏; Pisces—♓
7. d. Taurus—♉; Gemini—♊; Libra—♎
8. g. Sagittarius—♐; Capricorn—♑; Pisces—♓

EXERCISE 25
1. h. Gemini—♊; Virgo—♍; Capricorn—♑
2. c. Virgo—♍; Scorpio—♏; Aquarius—♒
3. g. Taurus—♉; Scorpio—♏; Capricorn—♑
4. d. Gemini—♊; Sagittarius—♐; Aquarius—♒
5. f. Leo—♌; Libra—♎; Scorpio—♏
6. b. Taurus—♉; Cancer—♋; Libra—♎
7. a. Libra—♎; Sagittarius—♐; Pisces—♓
8. e. Aries—♈; Scorpio—♏; Sagittarius—♐

EXERCISE 26
1. a. Aries—♈; Aquarius—♒; Pisces—♓
2. g. Gemini—♊; Scorpio—♏; Capricorn—♑
3. b. Taurus—♉; Cancer—♋; Scorpio—♏
4. e. Cancer—♋; Leo—♌; Pisces—♓
5. h. Aries—♈; Taurus—♉; Capricorn—♑
6. c. Cancer—♋; Libra—♎; Aquarius—♒
7. d. Virgo—♍; Sagittarius—♐; Capricorn—♑
8. f. Libra—♎; Capricorn—♑; Aquarius—♒

EXERCISE 27
- a. 10
- b. 7
- c. 1.
- d. 12
- e. 2
- f. 6
- g. 11
- h. 3
- i. 9
- j. 4
- k. 5
- l. 8

EXERCISE 28
1. l. Pisces (♓) in the first house
2. k. Aquarius (♒) in the fifth house
3. j. Capricorn (♑) in the tenth house
4. g. Libra (♎) in the fourth house
5. b. Taurus (♉) in the second house
6. f. Virgo (♍) in the third house
7. c. Gemini (♊) in the eleventh house
8. a. Aries (♈) in the seventh house
9. i. Sagittarius (♐) in the eighth house
10. h. Scorpio (♏) in the twelfth house
11. d. Cancer (♋) in the ninth house
12. e. Leo (♌) in the sixth house

EXERCISE 29
1. l. Pisces (♓) in the tenth house
2. a. Aries (♈) in the fourth house
3. b. Taurus (♉) in the eighth house
4. e. Leo (♌) in the second house
5. c. Gemini (♊) in the twelfth house
6. k. Aquarius (♒) in the seventh house
7. j. Capricorn (♑) in the first house
8. d. Cancer (♋) in the eleventh house
9. g. Libra (♎) in the sixth house
10. i. Sagittarius (♐) in the third house
11. h. Scorpio (♏) in the fifth house
12. f. Virgo (♍) in the ninth house

EXERCISE 30
1. l. Pisces (♓) in the eighth house
2. f. Virgo (♍) in the tenth house
3. a. Aries (♈) in the fifth house
4. k. Aquarius (♒) in the eleventh house
5. g. Libra (♎) in the second house
6. b. Taurus (♉) in the ninth house
7. i. Sagittarius (♐) in the twelfth house
8. c. Gemini (♊) in the third house
9. e. Leo (♌) in the seventh house
10. j. Capricorn (♑) in the fourth house
11. h. Scorpio (♏) in the sixth house
12. d. Cancer (♋) in the first house

EXERCISE 31
1. e. Leo (♌) in the eleventh house
2. a. Aries (♈) in the third house
3. l. Pisces (♓) in the ninth house
4. i. Sagittarius (♐) in the tenth house
5. h. Scorpio (♏) in the fourth house
6. b. Taurus (♉) in the sixth house
7. f. Virgo (♍) in the eighth house
8. j. Capricorn (♑) in the twelfth house
9. c. Gemini (♊) in the first house
10. g. Libra (♎) in the fifth house
11. d. Cancer (♋) in the seventh house
12. k. Aquarius (♒) in the second house

EXERCISE 32
1. k. Aquarius (♒) in the first house
2. a. Aries (♈) in the second house
3. e. Leo (♌) in the twelfth house
4. j. Capricorn (♑) in the third house
5. b. Taurus (♉) in the tenth house
6. g. Libra (♎) in the eighth house
7. i. Sagittarius (♐) in the fifth house
8. d. Cancer (♋) in the sixth house
9. h. Scorpio (♏) in the ninth house
10. l. Pisces (♓) in the eleventh house
11. c. Gemini (♊) in the seventh house
12. f. Virgo (♍) in the fourth house

EXERCISE 33
1. f. Virgo (♍) in the eleventh house
2. b. Taurus (♉) in the fourth house
3. l. Pisces (♓) in the sixth house
4. a. Aries (♈) in the eighth house
5. e. Leo (♌) in the third house
6. i. Sagittarius (♐) in the seventh house
7. h. Scorpio (♏) in the first house
8. g. Libra (♎) in the tenth house
9. d. Cancer (♋) in the fifth house
10. k. Aquarius (♒) in the twelfth house
11. c. Gemini (♊) in the second house
12. d. Capricorn (♑) in the ninth house

EXERCISE 34
1. l. Pisces (♓) in the twelfth house
2. a. Aries (♈) in the eleventh house
3. e. Leo (♌) in the tenth house
4. i. Sagittarius (♐) in the second house
5. b. Taurus (♉) in the first house
6. g. Libra (♎) in the third house
7. e. Capricorn (♑) in the sixth house
8. d. Cancer (♋) in the eighth house
9. h. Scorpio (♏) in the seventh house
10. k. Aquarius (♒) in the ninth house
11. c. Gemini (♊) in the fourth house
12. f. Virgo (♍) in the fifth house

EXERCISE 35
1. f. Virgo (♍) in the second house
2. e. Leo (♌) in the fourth house
3. a. Aries (♈) in the first house
4. l. Pisces (♓) in the fifth house
5. h. Scorpio (♏) in the eleventh house
6. c. Gemini (♊) in the ninth house
7. d. Cancer (♋) in the twelfth house
8. k. Aquarius (♒) in the tenth house
9. i. Sagittarius (♐) in the sixth house
10. g. Libra (♎) in the seventh house
11. j. Capricorn (♑) in the eighth house
12. b. Taurus (♉) in the third house

EXERCISE 36
1. e. Leo (♌) in the fifth house
2. j. Capricorn (♑) in the second house
3. k. Aquarius (♒) in the third house
4. i. Sagittarius (♐) in the fourth house
5. a. Aries (♈) in the sixth house
6. h. Scorpio (♏) in the third house
7. l. Pisces (♓) in the second house
8. g. Libra (♎) in the first house
9. b. Taurus (♉) in the fifth house
10. c. Gemini (♊) in the sixth house
11. d. Cancer (♋) in the fourth house
12. f. Virgo (♍) in the first house

EXERCISE 37
1. f. Virgo (♍) in the twelfth house
2. b. Taurus (♉) in the seventh house
3. k. Aquarius (♒) in the eighth house
4. d. Cancer (♋) in the tenth house
5. i. Sagittarius (♐) in the ninth house
6. g. Libra (♎) in the eleventh house
7. h. Scorpio (♏) in the tenth house
8. l. Pisces (♓) in the seventh house
9. e. Leo (♌) in the ninth house
10. j. Capricorn (♑) in the eleventh house
11. a. Aries (♈) in the twelfth house
12. c. Gemini (♊) in the eighth house

EXERCISE 38
1. b. Moon (☽)
2. d. Venus (♀)
3. j. Pluto (♇)
4. a. Sun (☉)
5. i. Neptune (♆)
6. f. Jupiter (♃)
7. h. Uranus (♅)
8. c. Mercury (☿)
9. g. Saturn (♄)
10. e. Mars (♂)

EXERCISE 39
1. b. Moon (☽) in the first house
2. e. Mars (♂) in the fourth house
3. g. Saturn (♄) in the second house
4. j. Pluto (♇) in the tenth house
5. d. Venus (♀) in the third house
6. i. Neptune (♆) in the seventh house
7. f. Jupiter (♃) in the sixth house
8. c. Mercury (☿) in the fifth house
9. a. Sun (☉) in the ninth house
10. h. Uranus (♅) in the eleventh house

EXERCISE 40
1. g. Saturn (♄) in the eighth house
2. h. Uranus (♅) in the seventh house
3. b. Moon (☽) in the tenth house
4. j. Pluto (♇) in the third house
5. i. Neptune (♆) in the first house
6. f. Jupiter (♃) in the eleventh house
7. e. Mars (♂) in the sixth house
8. d. Venus (♀) in the fifth house
9. c. Mercury (☿) in the twelfth house
10. a. Sun (☉) in the fourth house

EXERCISE 41
1. e. Mars (♂) in the first house
2. j. Pluto (♇) in the seventh house
3. a. Sun (☉) in the fifth house
4. i. Neptune (♆) in the fourth house
5. b. Moon (☽) in the second house
6. g. Saturn (♄) in the sixth house
7. c. Mercury (☿) in the tenth house
8. h. Uranus (♅) in the third house
9. f. Jupiter (♃) in the eighth house
10. d. Venus (♀) in the eleventh house

EXERCISE 42
1. d. Venus (♀) in the second house
2. j. Pluto (♇) in the sixth house
3. a. Sun (☉) in the first house
4. g. Saturn (♄) in the fourth house
5. i. Neptune (♆) in the sixth house
6. b. Moon (☽) in the third house
7. h. Uranus (♅) in the fifth house
8. c. Mercury (☿) in the first house
9. e. Mars (♂) in the third house
10. f. Jupiter (♃) in the fifth house

EXERCISE 43
1. c. Mercury (☿) in the ninth house
2. j. Pluto (♇) in the eleventh house
3. h. Uranus (♅) in the twelfth house
4. a. Sun (☉) in the seventh house
5. g. Saturn (♄) in the ninth house
6. f. Jupiter (♃) in the twelfth house
7. d. Venus (♀) in the tenth house
8. i. Neptune (♆) in the eighth house
9. b. Moon (☽) in the eleventh house
10. e. Mars (♂) in the eighth house

EXERCISE 44
1. g. Saturn (♄) in the fifth house
2. j. Pluto (♇) in the first house
3. c. Mercury (☿) in the third house
4. d. Venus (♀) in the first house
5. i. Neptune (♆) in the third house
6. a. Sun (☉) in the third house
7. h. Uranus (♅) in the first house
8. f. Jupiter (♃) in the first house
9. e. Mars (♂) in the fifth house
10. b. Moon (☽) in the fifth house

EXERCISE 45
1. e. Mars (♂) in the eleventh house
2. j. Pluto (♇) in the ninth house
3. f. Jupiter (♃) in the seventh house
4. a. Sun (☉) in the eleventh house
5. d. Venus (♀) in the ninth house
6. b. Moon (☽) in the seventh house
7. c. Mercury (☿) in the eleventh house
8. h. Uranus (♅) in the ninth house
9. i. Neptune (♆) in the eleventh house
10. g. Saturn (♄) in the seventh house

EXERCISE 46
1. f. Jupiter (♃) in the fourth house
2. i. Neptune (♆) in the twelfth house
3. g. Saturn (♄) in the tenth house
4. b. Moon (☽) in the fourth house
5. d. Venus (♀) in the sixth house
6. j. Pluto (♇) in the eighth house
7. e. Mars (♂) in the second house
8. a. Sun (☉) in the sixth house
9. c. Mercury (☿) in the second house
10. h. Uranus (♅) in the eighth house

EXERCISE 47
1. h. Uranus (♅) in Taurus (♉) in the ninth house
2. e. Mars (♂) in Aries (♈) in the seventh house
3. d. Venus (♀) in Capricorn (♑) in the fourth house
4. g. Saturn (♄) in Pisces (♓) in the first house
5. j. Pluto (♇) in Cancer (♋) in the eighth house
6. i. Neptune (♆) in Virgo (♍) in the third house
7. c. Mercury (☿) in Leo (♌) in the tenth house
8. a. Sun (☉) in Scorpio (♏) in the eleventh house
9. b. Moon (☽) in Libra (♎) in the sixth house
10. f. Jupiter (♃) in Gemini (♊) in the second house

EXERCISE 48
1. f. Jupiter (♃) in Gemini (♊) in sixth house
2. a. Sun (☉) in Aquarius (♒) in the twelfth house
3. i. Neptune (♆) in Libra (♎) in the seventh house
4. c. Mercury (☿) in Aries (♈) in the third house
5. j. Pluto (♀) in Leo (♌) in the ninth house
6. h. Uranus (♅) in Leo (♌) in the first house
7. g. Saturn (♄) in Cancer (♋) in the eighth house
8. e. Mars (♂) in Virgo (♍) in the fifth house
9. d. Venus (♀) in Taurus (♉) in the second house
10. b. Moon (☽) in Pisces (♓) in the eleventh house

EXERCISE 49
1. j. Pluto (♀) in Libra (♎) in the second house
2. c. Mercury (☿) in Sagittarius (♐) in the fifth house
3. g. Saturn (♄) in Virgo (♍) in the sixth house
4. a. Sun (☉) in Aries (♈) in the fourth house
5. f. Jupiter (♃) in Pisces (♓) in the eleventh house
6. i. Neptune (♆) in Leo (♌) in the first house
7. b. Moon (☽) in Scorpio (♏) in the twelfth house
8. d. Venus (♀) in Aquarius (♒) in the eighth house
9. e. Mars (♂) in Taurus (♉) in the third house
10. h. Uranus (♅) in Cancer (♋) in the seventh house

EXERCISE 50
1. e. Mars (♂) in Pisces (♓) in the eighth house
2. d. Venus (♀) in Sagittarius (♐) in the ninth house
3. j. Pluto (♀) in Virgo (♍) in the twelfth house
4. a. Sun (☉) in Cancer (♋) in the first house
5. b. Moon (☽) in Aquarius (♒) in the fifth house
6. g. Saturn (♄) in Scorpio (♏) in the third house
7. i. Neptune (♆) in Gemini (♊) in the tenth house
8. c. Mercury (☿) in Libra (♎) in the eleventh house
9. f. Jupiter (♃) in Taurus (♉) in the seventh house
10. h. Uranus (♅) in Aries (♈) in the fourth house

EXERCISE 51
1. d. Venus (♀) in Pisces (♓) in the tenth house
2. j. Pluto (♀︎) in Scorpio (♏) in the eleventh house
3. a. Sun (☉) in Gemini (♊) in the fifth house
4. i. Neptune (♆) in Cancer (♋) in the second house
5. g. Saturn (♄) in Aquarius (♒) in the seventh house
6. e. Mars (♂) in Leo (♌) in the sixth house
7. b. Moon (☽) in Aries (♈) in the first house
8. h. Uranus (♅) in Taurus (♉) in the fourth house
9. c. Mercury (☿) in Sagittarius (♐) in the twelfth house
10. f. Jupiter (♃) in Virgo (♍) in the eighth house

EXERCISE 52
1. f. Jupiter (♃) in Cancer (♋) in the third house
2. e. Mars (♂) in Capricorn (♑) in the ninth house
3. a. Sun (☉) in Virgo (♍) in the seventh house
4. h. Uranus (♅) in Gemini (♊) in the sixth house
5. b. Moon (☽) in Leo (♌) in the tenth house
6. j. Pluto (♀︎) in Cancer (♋) in the fourth house
7. d. Venus (♀) in Aries (♈) in the first house
8. g. Saturn (♄) in Sagittarius (♐) in the fifth house
9. i. Neptune (♆) in Scorpio (♏) in the twelfth house
10. c. Mercury (☿) in Scorpio (♏) in the second house

EXERCISE 53
1. e. Mars (♂) in Gemini (♊) in the eleventh house
2. a. Sun (☉) in Capricorn (♑) in the tenth house
3. j. Pluto (♀︎) in Gemini (♊) in the sixth house
4. f. Jupiter (♃) in Libra (♎) in the twelfth house
5. b. Moon (☽) in Taurus (♉) in the third house
6. i. Neptune (♆) in Sagittarius (♐) in the fifth house
7. c. Mercury (☿) in Cancer (♋) in the first house
8. g. Saturn (♄) in Aries (♈) in the ninth house
9. d. Venus (♀) in Leo (♌) in the seventh house
10. h. Uranus (♅) in Scorpio (♏) in the eighth house

EXERCISE 54
1. i. Neptune (Ψ) in Leo (Ω) in the eighth house
2. d. Venus ($♀$) in Virgo ($\mathfrak{M}$) in the eleventh house
3. f. Jupiter ($♃$) in Aries ($♈$) in the first house
4. b. Moon ($☽$) in Capricorn ($♑$) in the fourth house
5. j. Pluto ($♇$) in Leo (Ω) in the seventh house
6. e. Mars ($♂$) in Scorpio ($\mathfrak{M}$) in the tenth house
7. a. Sun ($☉$) in Pisces ($♓$) in the sixth house
8. g. Saturn ($♄$) in Libra ($♎$) in the second house
9. h. Uranus ($♅$) in Virgo ($\mathfrak{M}$) in the fifth house
10. c. Mercury ($☿$) in Aquarius ($♒$) in the ninth house

EXERCISE 55
1. d. Moon ($☽$)-Pluto ($♇$)
2. g. Venus ($♀$)-Saturn ($♄$)
3. h. Mars ($♂$)-Neptune (Ψ)
4. b. Sun ($☉$)-Jupiter ($♃$)
5. e. Mercury ($☿$)-Uranus ($♅$)
6. j. Neptune (Ψ)-Pluto ($♇$)
7. f. Venus ($♀$)-Mars ($♂$)
8. c. Moon ($☽$)-Uranus ($♅$)
9. i. Jupiter ($♃$)-Saturn ($♄$)
10. a. Sun ($☉$)-Mercury ($☿$)

EXERCISE 56
1. i. Mars ($♂$)-Uranus ($♅$)
2. e. Mercury ($☿$)-Jupiter ($♃$)
3. b. Sun ($☉$)-Saturn ($♄$)
4. d. Moon ($☽$)-Neptune (Ψ)
5. j. Uranus ($♅$)-Pluto ($♇$)
6. g. Venus ($♀$)-Neptune (Ψ)
7. a. Sun ($☉$)-Mars ($♂$)
8. f. Mercury ($☿$)-Saturn ($♄$)
9. c. Moon ($☽$)-Jupiter ($♃$)
10. h. Venus ($♀$)-Pluto ($♇$)

EXERCISE 57
1. d. Mercury ($☿$)-Venus ($♀$)
2. f. Venus ($♀$)-Uranus ($♅$)
3. c. Moon ($☽$)-Mars ($♂$)
4. g. Mars ($♂$)-Jupiter ($♃$)
5. b. Sun ($☉$)-Pluto ($♇$)
6. e. Mercury ($☿$)-Neptune (Ψ)
7. h. Jupiter ($♃$)-Uranus ($♅$)
8. a. Sun ($☉$)-Moon ($☽$)
9. i. Saturn ($♄$)-Neptune (Ψ)
10. j. Saturn ($♄$)-Pluto ($♇$)

EXERCISE 58
1. f. Mercury ($☿$)-Mars ($♂$)
2. i. Jupiter ($♃$)-Neptune (Ψ)
3. c. Sun ($☉$)-Neptune (Ψ)
4. d. Moon ($☽$)-Mercury ($☿$)
5. a. Sun ($☉$)-Venus ($♀$)
6. h. Mars ($♂$)-Pluto ($♇$)
7. b. Sun ($☉$)-Uranus ($♅$)
8. g. Mars ($♂$)-Saturn ($♄$)
9. j. Saturn ($♄$)-Uranus ($♅$)
10. e. Moon ($☽$)-Venus ($♀$)

EXERCISE 59
1. j. Pluto (♇)-Nodes (☊☋)
2. b. Moon (☽)-Nodes (☊☋)
3. f. Jupiter (♃)-Nodes (☊☋)
4. i. Neptune (♆)-Nodes (☊☋)
5. a. Sun (☉)-Nodes (☊☋)
6. d. Venus (♀)-Nodes (☊☋)
7. g. Saturn (♄)-Nodes (☊☋)
8. e. Mars (♂)-Nodes (☊☋)
9. c. Mercury (☿)-Nodes (☊☋)
10. h. Uranus (♅)-Nodes (☊☋)

EXERCISE 60
1. i. Neptune (♆)-MC
2. e. Mars (♂)-MC
3. h. Uranus (♅)-MC
4. b. Moon (☽)-MC
5. d. Venus (♀)-MC
6. g. Saturn (♄)-MC
7. a. Sun (☉)-MC
8. f. Jupiter (♃)-MC
9. c. Mercury (☿)-MC
10. j. Pluto (♇)-MC

EXERCISE 61
1. g. Saturn (♄)-Asc.
2. d. Venus (♀)-Asc.
3. f. Jupiter (♃)-Asc.
4. a. Sun (☉)-Asc.
5. e. Mars (♂)-Asc.
6. b. Moon (☽)-Asc.
7. i. Neptune (♆)-Asc.
8. c. Mercury (☿)-Asc.
9. h. Uranus (♅)-Asc.
10. j. Pluto (♇)-Asc.

EXERCISE 62
1. i. Yod
2. f. T-Square or Grand Cross in fixed signs
3. c. Grand Trine in air
4. h. Cradle
5. b. Grand Trine in earth
6. e. T-Square or Grand Cross in cardinal signs
7. a. Grand Trine in fire
8. d. Grand Trine in water
9. g. T-Square or Grand Cross in mutable signs

EXERCISE 63
1. c. Venus (♀)-Uranus (♅)-Neptune (♆)
2. b. Moon (☽)-Mercury (☿)-Asc.
3. d. Mars (♂)-Jupiter (♃)-Pluto (♇)
4. c. Venus (♀)-Uranus (♅)-Neptune (♆)
5. a. Sun (☉)-Moon (☽)-Saturn (♄)
6. b. Moon (☽)-Mercury (☿)-Asc.
7. d. Mars (♂)-Jupiter (♃)-Pluto (♇)
8. a. Sun (☉)-Moon (☽)-Saturn (♄)

EXERCISE 64
1. c. Moon (☽)-Venus (♀)-Asc.
2. a. Sun (☉)-Pluto (♇)-MC
3. d. Mars (♂)-Saturn (♄)-Uranus (♅)
4. b. Mercury (☿)-Jupiter (♃)-Neptune (♆)
5. b. Mercury (☿)-Jupiter (♃)-Neptune (♆)
6. a. Sun (☉)-Pluto (♇)-MC
7. c. Moon (☽)-Venus (♀)-Asc.
8. d. Mars (♂)-Saturn (♄)-Uranus (♅)

EXERCISE 65
1. d. Mercury (☿)-Saturn (♄)-Pluto (♇)
2. b. Moon (☽)-Uranus (♅)-MC
3. c. Venus (♀)-Mars (♂)-Jupiter (♃)
4. a. Sun (☉)-Mars (♂)-Neptune (♆)
5. a. Sun (☉)-Mars (♂)-Neptune (♆)
6. b. Moon (☽)-Uranus (♅)-MC
7. c. Venus (♀)-Mars (♂)-Jupiter (♃)
8. d. Mercury (☿)-Saturn (♄)-Pluto (♇)

EXERCISE 66
1. d. Moon (☽)-Pluto (♇)-MC
2. a. Sun (☉)-Jupiter (♃)-Uranus (♅)
3. c. Venus (♀)-Saturn (♄)-Pluto (♇)
4. b. Mercury (☿)-Mars (♂)-Neptune (♆)
5. c. Venus (♀)-Saturn (♄)-Pluto (♇)
6. a. Sun (☉)-Jupiter (♃)-Uranus (♅)
7. d. Moon (☽)-Pluto (♇)-MC
8. b. Mercury (☿)-Mars (♂)-Neptune (♆)

EXERCISES 67-75
The charts used in these exercises are those of Dustin Hoffman, Liza Minnelli, and Charles Manson.

CHART A	CHART B	CHART C
Dustin Hoffman	Liza Minnelli	Charles Manson
Aug. 8, 1937	March 12, 1946	Nov. 12, 1934
17:07 hrs. P.S.T.	07:58 hrs. P.S.T.	16:40 hrs. E.S.T.
Los Angeles, Cal.	Los Angeles, Cal.	Cincinnati, Ohio

EXERCISE 67
1. B.
2. C.
3. A.

EXERCISE 68
1. D.   4. B.   7. B.
2. C.   5. D.   8. A.
3. A.   6. C.

EXERCISE 69
1. C.   4. C.
2. A.   5. A.
3. B.   6. B.

EXERCISE 70
1. C. Chart C—(a) Capricorn (♑) and Aquarius (♒); (b) Moon (☽) in the tenth house, North Node (☊) in the tenth house and conjunct each other; (c) Grand Cross involving Moon (☽) conjunct North Node (☊) opposition South Node (☋) and Pluto (♇), and square Ascendant on one side and Mercury (☿) conjunct Jupiter (♃) on the other; (d) Moon (☽) and North Node (☊) opposition Pluto (♇) and square Mercury (☿) on one side and Uranus (♅) on the other.
2. A. Chart A—(a) Scorpio (♏) and Aquarius (♒); (b) Mars (♂) in Sagittarius (♐) in the tenth house; (c) Mars (♂) is part of a Grand Trine with Saturn (♄) and Pluto (♇); (d) same Grand Trine; (e) Mars (♂) quintile Neptune (♆) and Moon (☽) and bi-quintile Venus (♀).
3. B. Chart B—(a) Capricorn (♑); (b) Aquarius (♒); (c) Capricorn (♑); (d) Aquarius (♒); (e) Capricorn (♑); (f) Capricorn (♑); (g) Aquarius (♒); (h) Aquarius (♒).

EXERCISE 71
1. B. Chart B—(a) Saturn (♄), ruler of the tenth house, is in the third house; (b) Saturn (♄) trine Sun (☉); (c) Saturn (♄) conjunct Mars (♂) and Moon (☽), square Jupiter (♃) and opposition MC; (d) same as (c).
2. A. Chart A—(a) Mars (♂) in the tenth house and Pluto (♇) in the seventh house; (b) Mars (♂) and Pluto (♇) trine each other, and both trine Saturn (♄), forming a Grand Trine; (c) Mars (♂) quintile Moon (☽) and Neptune (♆) and bi-quintile Venus (♀); (d) Pluto (♇) sesqui-quadrate North Node (☊) but trine Saturn (♄).
3. C. Chart C—(a) Saturn (♄) is in the eleventh house; (b) Saturn (♄) square the Sun (☉)-Venus (♀) conjunction; (c) Saturn (♄) quintile Ascendant; (d) Saturn (♄) sextile Uranus (♅); (e) Saturn (♄) semi-sextile MC.

EXERCISE 72
1. A. Chart A—(a) Cancer (♋); (b) Leo (♌); (c) Sun (☉) and also Pluto (♇) in the house; (d) Sun (☉) in Leo (♌) in the seventh house and Pluto (♇) in the house and part of the Grand Trine with Mars (♂) and Saturn (♄); (e) Pluto (♇) sesqui-quadrate North Node (☊); (f) Sun (☉) in the seventh house, opposition Part of Fortune (⊗); (g) Sun (☉) square Uranus (♅) and semi-sextile Moon (☽) and Neptune (♆); (h) Sun (☉) trine North Node (☊).
2. C. Chart C—(a) Scorpio (♏); (b) Sagittarius (♐); (c) Jupiter (♃), Sun (☉) and Venus (♀) in the seventh house, and Sun (☉) trine the Part of Fortune (⊗); (d) Grand Cross involving Jupiter (♃), Mercury (☿), Ascendant, Moon (☽), North Node (☊) and South Node (☋); (e) same Grand Cross; (f) Jupiter (♃) quintile MC, sextile Neptune (♆) and Mars (♂); (g) Sun (☉) conjunct Venus (♀), sextile Neptune (♆), but square Saturn (♄); (h) Sun (☉) conjunct Venus (♀), sextile MC, trine Pluto (♇) and sextile Mars (♂).
3. B. Chart B—(a) Scorpio (♏); (b) Scorpio (♏); (c) Sagittarius (♐); (d) Scorpio (♏); (e) Sagittarius (♐).

EXERCISE 73
1. B. Chart B—(a) Mars (♂), co-ruler of the seventh house is in the third house; (b) Pluto (♀), co-ruler of the seventh house, is in the fourth house; (c) Mars (♂) trine Sun (☉); (d) Mars (♂) conjunct Saturn (♄); (e) Pluto (♀) trine Mercury (☿); (f) Mars (♂) conjunct Moon (☽) (g) Mars (♂) conjunct Saturn (♄); (h) Mars (♂) opposition MC; (i) Pluto (♀) semi-square North Node (☊); (j) Pluto (♀) sextile Neptune (♆); (k) Pluto (♀) sextile Uranus (♅).
2. C. Chart C—(a) Pluto (♀), co-ruler of the seventh house, is in the fourth house; (b) Mars (♂), co-ruler of the seventh house, is in the fifth house; (c) Mars (♂) conjunct Neptune (♆), sextile Sun (☉) and Venus (♀) and sesqui-quadrate Uranus (♅); (d) Pluto (♀) conjunct Part of Fortune (⊗) and trine Sun (☉) and Venus (♀) in the seventh house; (e) Pluto (♀) conjunct South Node (☋), opposition North Node (☊)-Moon (☽) conjunction, square Mercury (☿) and Uranus (♅) and opposition MC.
3. A. Chart A—(a) Moon (☽), ruler of the seventh house, is in the eighth house, in a water house and in an earth sign, also the Moon (☽) is part of an earth Grand Trine; (b) Moon (☽) squares the Nodes (☊☋); (c) Moon (☽) conjunct Neptune (♆); (d) Moon (☽) quintiles Mars (♂) and Venus (♀), conjuncts Mercury (☿) and trines Uranus (♅); (e) earth Grand Trine, including Moon (☽), Jupiter (♃) and Uranus (♅).

EXERCISE 74
1. B. Chart B—(a) Cancer (♋); (b) Leo (♌); (c) Pluto (♇) in the fourth house; (d) Pluto (♇) semi-square North Node (☊); (e) Pluto (♇) sextile Neptune (♆); (f) Pluto (♇) trine Mercury (☿); (g) Pluto (♇) sextile Uranus (♅).
2. C. Chart C—(a) Cancer (♋) in the fourth house; (b) Leo (♌) in the fourth house; (c) Pluto (♇) in the fourth house; (d) Pluto (♇) square Uranus (♅), trine Sun (☉) and Venus (♀); (e) South Node (☋) in the fourth house and part of a Grand Cross; (f) Pluto (♇) opposition Moon (☽), MC and North Node (☊) and conjunct Part of Fortune (⊗); (g) South Node (☋) square the Mercury (☿)-Jupiter (♃) conjunction, opposition Moon (☽) and North Node (☊) and square Ascendant.
3. A. Chart A—(a) Taurus (♉) in the fourth house; (b) Gemini (♊) in the fourth house; (c) Uranus (♅) in the fourth house; (d) Uranus (♅), part of a T-Square, is square Part of Fortune (⊗) on one side and Sun (☉) in the seventh house on the other; (e) Uranus (♅) quincunx North Node (☊); (f) Uranus (♅) is part of an earth Grand Trine; (g) Taurus (♉) in the fourth house, and the Grand Trine in earth; (h) Uranus (♅) trine Ascendant and Mercury (☿); (i) Uranus (♅) trine Moon (☽) and Jupiter (♃); (j) Uranus (♅) trine Neptune (♆).

EXERCISE 75
1. A. Chart A—(a) Venus (♀), ruler of the fourth house is in the sixth house; (b) Venus (♀) square Saturn (♄); (c) most aspects to Venus (♀) are soft; (d) Venus (♀) quintile Neptune (♆); (e) Venus (♀) quintile Moon (☽); (f) Venus (♀) sextile Mercury (☿), which is conjunct Moon (☽) and Neptune (♆); (g) Venus (♀) bi-quintile Mars (♂) and trine MC; (h) Venus (♀) sesqui-quadrate Part of Fortune (⊗).
2. C. Chart C—(a) Moon (☽), ruler of the fourth house, is in the tenth house; (b) Moon (☽) is part of a fixed Grand Cross; (c) Moon (☽) in the tenth house conjuncts North Node (☊) and opposes South Node (☋); (d) Moon (☽) is square Ascendant; (e) Moon (☽) square Mercury (☿) conjunct Jupiter (♃); (f) Moon (☽) conjunct North Node (☊), opposition South Node (☋) and square Ascendant; (g) Moon (☽) square Uranus (♅) and opposition Pluto (♇).
3. B. Chart B—(a) Moon (☽), ruler of the fourth house, is in the third house; (b) Moon (☽) is ruler of the fourth house and in the third house; (c) Moon (☽) conjunct Mars (♂); (d) Moon (☽) conjunct Saturn (♄); (e) Moon (☽) conjunct Mars (♂) and square Jupiter (♃); (f) Moon (☽) opposition MC; (g) Moon (☽) trine Sun (☉).

EXERCISE 76

Martin Luther King was a practical (♑♉), ambitious (♑) man with a great deal of persistence (♑♉). He had a strong sense of duty (♑) which, when coupled with his compassion (♓), gave him the ability to sacrifice himself (♓) in the service of others (♍). The practicality (all three earth signs represented) and persistence (♉♍♑) are strongly emphasized as is the emotional side (♓♍) of his character.

He was also a visionary (♒) and dreamer (♓) who could use his more down-to-earth (♉♍♑) qualities to accomplish tangible results (♉♍♑) in humanitarian causes (♒).

EXERCISE 77

1. He could utilize spirituality (♆) and philosophy (♃) easily (Grand Trine) in a practical way (♄ and earth) with great enthusiasm (fire).
2. His emotions (☽) might inhibit (♄) his taking action (♂), or the emotions (☽) could direct (♄) his actions (♂).
3. He might be deceived (♆) in relationships (☊☋), or he might relate (☊☋) to spiritual (♆) people.

EXERCISE 78

King would need a career that required discipline (♑) but allowed for a degree of independence (♒) as well. He would be responsible and duty-oriented (♑) and might choose a profession involving humanitarian causes (♒).

Communications, particularly with peers or large groups (♒ and ☿ in ♒ in the tenth house), would be essential. King might communicate artistically (♀ semi-sextile ☿) with originality (♀ in ♒ and sextile ♅). His practicality (Ascendant in ♉, square ☿), however, might inhibit the flow of creative communications (♄ semi-square ☿ in ♒) regarding the career.

EXERCISE 79

Professionally King might utilize other people's resources or have an interest in transformation and regeneration (♄ in the eighth house). The emotions (☽) could restrict (square ♄) his initiative (square ♂), or he might act (♂) emotionally (☽) regarding restrictions (♄). He could also have problems with communications (♄ semi-square ☿) in this area. If, however, he considered his goals and what would give him ego gratification (♄ semi-sextile ☉) this would help. But more importantly, if he utilized his sensitivity or spiritual tendencies (♆ trine ♄) and operated religiously and philosophically (♃ trine ♄) the problems could be alleviated.

EXERCISE 80

Martin Luther King was deeply emotional in the area of partnership or needed a partner who was deeply emotional (♍). He also preferred one who was warm and outgoing, and with whom he could develop and grow (♐). He could have been loyal to, and perhaps possessive of, the partner (♍), but he would have wanted someone who was free enough to grow philosophically or religiously (♐).

He felt a strong sense of responsibility (☋ in the seventh house having a Saturnian quality) regarding his wife, and related to others with her (☋ opposition ☊ in the first and seventh houses). His public image (MC sextile ☋) might be enhanced, and ego needs (☉ sextile ☋) gratified, through relationships developed with the partner. He and his wife should have been careful about being deceived or taken advantage of by others (♆ square ☋) and might have avoided problems of this sort by association with spiritually inclined people (♆). They also would have had the ability to change relationships suddenly (☋ trine ☋), if difficulties arose.

EXERCISE 81

King needed to feel materially secure with the partner (♂, co-ruler of the seventh house, in the second house) and to take action (♂) both to provide security and to receive it. The ability to communicate (♀, co-ruler of the seventh house, in the third house) with the partner, on both a superficial level (third house) and in a deep manner (♀), was essential. Action and initiating (♂) in partnership might sometimes (mutable T-Square) be restricted (♂ opposition ♄) by the emotions (☽ square ♂) or sometimes based on disciplining (♄) the emotions (☽). When the public image (MC) was considered, action could be more easily taken (MC bi-quintile ♂).

Intense and vigorous communications (♀ in the third house) with the partner or through the partnership would need to be balanced with the ego needs (♀ opposition ☉) and might sometimes be misunderstood (♆ semi-square ♀). However, when the emotional needs (☽ trine ♀) of the other person were considered and this consideration was expressed directly through the personality (Ascendant sextile ♀), communicating could be very enjoyable (♀ trine ♀).

EXERCISE 82

Martin Luther King communicated in an emotional manner (♋). His speech was powerful and effective (♀), and writing and speaking could give him a sense of fulfillment (⊗). He would easily feel a sense of satisfaction (⊗) when artistically (sextile ♀) expressing his own point of view (sextile Ascendant) on philosophy (sextile ♃) and spiritual matters (sextile ♆). His communications might, however, seem too liberal (square ♅) to some.

The need for power (♀) through communications might interfere with his ego gratification (opposition ☉) because he might be misunderstood (semi-square ♆), but he would make a pleasurable (trine ♀) impression (sextile Ascendant) when expressing his emotions (trine ☽).

EXERCISE 83

He often found himself speaking to large groups (☽, the ruler of the third house, is in the eleventh house). He could express himself (☽ sextile ☉), and make a good impression on these groups (sextile Ascendant) and easily exercise power (☽ trine ♀) in this way. His public speaking, however, might sometimes (mutable T-Square) interfere with (square ♄) his taking action (square ♂).

EXERCISE 84

Eleanor Roosevelt was a warm, outgoing and, at times, candid individual. She had an interest in foreign affairs and distant travel (♐). Her candor was tempered with tact and a desire for peace and harmony (♎). She was a sociable person (♊) and communications were essential to her (♊♎). She also tended to be motherly and protective of others (♋).

EXERCISE 85

1. Her initiative (♂) could be dissipated (♆) by attempting too much (♃), or her initiative (♂) could be utilized for great (♃) projects to help others (♆).
2. Her personality (Ascendant) might be restricted (♄) in attaining personal fulfillment (⊗), or she could attain fulfillment (⊗) by seriously (♄) applying herself (Ascendant).
3. A Cradle indicates help coming from others or the native's sometimes being in the right place at the right time. With the planets and points involved she might have had help from the action (♂) of the public or women (☽) to obtain spiritual (♆) fulfillment (⊗).
4. Her vital energy would be expressed in relationships (☉ conjunct ☊), but she might have had difficulty satisfying her ego needs (☉) through others because of deep emotional involvement and desire to protect those with whom she was involved (☉ and ☊ ☋ square ☽).

EXERCISE 86

The ninth house signifies not only distant travel, but also higher education, religion, publishing, etc. Keep in mind the particular definition of the area that is being investigated, and interpret within that framework. In Exercises 86 and 87 the ninth house will be delineated in terms of distant travel. In Exercises 88 and 89 the same house will be explored in terms of publishing, since Eleanor Roosevelt was an authoress as well as a world-traveler.

Eleanor Roosevelt traveled to foreign countries to serve others (♍).She also traveled to attain peace and harmony (♎). Her trips were for practical reasons, and the details were probably well-planned (♍). She undoubtedly had a traveling companion with whom she could have shared her experiences (♎).

She must have enjoyed her trips greatly (♀ conjunct ♃) and attained a sense of fulfillment (⊗) from them. Her journeys might have occurred unexpectedly (♅), or she could have expressed original or unusual ideas in foreign affairs (☿ conjunct ♅). Her communications and travels were often connected with her career (☿ conjunct ♅ and MC).

Expressing power (♀ square ♀) would have interfered with her pleasure (♀ conjunct ♃), and her ego (♀ semi-square ☉) and emotional needs (♀ semi-square ☽) might have been difficult to gratify under such circumstances.

She probably had difficulty at times in experiencing personal fulfillment because of inhibitions or a strong sense of responsibility (mutable T-Square: ⊗ square ♄ and Ascendant). Help toward a feeling of wholeness or fulfillment could have come through the action of others and given her spiritual and emotional (Cradle: ⊗ sextile ♂ and ☽ and trine ♆), as well as ego gratification (⊗ semi-sextile ☉).

Although ideas expressed in foreign affairs might have been non-conforming (☿ conjunct ♅), she could control these ideas (☿ conjunct ♅ and square ♄)and converse charmingly (☿ semi-sextile ♀), powerfully (♅ conjunct ☿ ,trine ♀) and fluently with the public (☿ conjunct ♅ and quintile ☽), in a professional capacity (☿ conjunct ♅ and MC). Such communication would have given her great (♅ semi-sextile ♃) spiritual (♅ trine ♆) satisfaction.

EXERCISE 87

The house of distant travel was strongly emphasized in Eleanor Roosevelt's life (☿, ruler of the ninth house, is in the ninth house), and communicating would definitely be important in this area (☿, the planet of communications, rules the house and is in the house). (The aspects to Mercury and interpretations thereof are given in Exercise 86.)

EXERCISE 88

Eleanor Roosevelt wrote factual and detail-oriented books (♍) in an aristic style (♎). It seems inevtitable that she would have talent in writing (☿ and ♀ are both in the ninth house and rule the two signs that are in the house, as well as being semi-sextile each other). She publicized creative ideas (♅ in the ninth house) and achieved fulfillment (⊗ in the ninth house) through publishing. The pleasure she received from writing is obvious (♀ conjunct ♃), but she painstakingly analyzed (♀ square ♀)her own ego needs (♀ semi-square ☉) and her emotions (♀ semi-square ☽)in her books. She had to exert discipline and effort to attain personal fulfillment (T-Square of ⊗ square Ascendant on one side and ♄ on the other). Public response, however, could stimulate her imaginative ability in writing and provide the energy to continue her work and attain personal fulfillment through her efforts (Cradle, including ⊗ sextile ♂ and ☽ and trine ♆).

(Every single aspect to each planet and point in the house has not been mentioned because mentioning each one would only be repetitive. The repetition strongly emphasizes the themes already expressed.)

EXERCISE 89

Mercury (☿), the ruler of the ninth house, being in the ninth house and also being the planet of communications reiterates the themes mentioned in Exercise 88. There are also a number of indications that Eleanor Roosevelt would share her works with the world (☿ in ♎,conjunct the MC; ♀, the ruler of the tenth house, is in the ninth house, etc.).

EXERCISE 90

Eleanor Roosevelt needed a partner with versatility and sociability with whom she could communicate (♊). She also needed a partner who would mother and protect her, or whom she could mother and protect (♋).

There was a strong sense of responsibility for the partner (♄ in the seventh house), accompanied by mothering qualities (☽ in ♋ in the seventh house). And she could have felt emotionally burdened at times in this area (♄ and ☽ in the seventh house).

This sense of responsibility for the partner sometimes interfered with her own need for personal fulfillment (mutable T-Square: ♄ opposition Ascendant and square ⊗) and restricted expression of her individuality (♄ square ☿ conjunct ♅). If, however, she could feel that she was sacrificing (♄ semi-sextile ♆) for the partner, she could easily initiate in his behalf (♄ bi-quintile ♂) and feel great (♄ sextile ♃) ego gratification (♄ trine ☉).

The emotional attachment to the partner might also conflict with ego needs (☽ square ☉) in relationships with others (☽ square ☊☿☋). On the other hand, the partner could offer opportunities (☽ part of the Cradle) to take action (☽ trine ♂) to serve others (☽ sextile ♆), providing self-fulfillment (☽ sextile ⊗).

EXERCISE 91

Eleanor Roosevelt needed to communicate with the partner on both the mundane and philosophical level. She could also have traveled to distant countries with the partner (☿, the planet of communications, rules the seventh house and is in the ninth house).

Initially she might have felt inhibited (☿ square ♄) in initiating communications with the partner or in opportunities provided by the partnership (☿ semi-square ♂). Eventually she would graciously express (☿ semi-sextile ♀) her deeper personal feelings (☿ quintile ☽ and Ascendant) creatively (☿ conjunct ♅) and exert power (☿ trine ♀) in this way in the world (☿ conjunct MC).

151

EXERCISE 92

Babe Ruth was a highly emotional individual (♋ and ♓) who could be protective of and self-sacrificing for those he cared about (♋ and ♓). He was also warm and outgoing (♐). Although he had sensitivity toward people he was close to (♋ and ♓), he was at times frank and outspoken (♐). His athletic prowess as well was shown by the Sagittarius emphasis.

He could be sociable (♊) and adaptable (three of the four mutable signs are represented), but he was an individualist and had a strong need for independence (♒); therefore, at times he was compliant and at other times non-conforming.

EXERCISE 93
1. He used his physical energy (♂) in an unusual and creative way (♅) to attain fulfillment (⊗) and ego gratification (☉); or he had a quick temper (♂ square ☉) which could erupt suddenly (♂ opposition ♅) and interfere with his fulfillment (⊗).
2. He was highly emotional (Grand Trine in water) and could receive pleasure (♀) by expressing (☿) his feelings (☽ and water) to the public (☽) in a disciplined manner (♄) through career (MC); or he might not have restrained (♄) the expression (☿) of his emotions (☽ and water) in the world (MC), when his pleasure (♀) was involved.
3. He was too generous in his relationships (♃ square ☊ ☋); or he involved himself in relationships that helped him to grow and develop. The fact that so many of his relationships were with other athletes fits this symbolism as well.

EXERCISE 94

In athletics Babe Ruth was individualistic and creative (♒) but strongly emotionally involved as well (♓). He needed a degree of independence in sports (♒) but also would deeply empathize and cooperate with others (♓).

He could directly manifest his vital energy and receive ego gratification through athletics (☉). He was talented (♀) in this area and could express himself there to the world (☿ conjunct MC).

His quick temper could erupt suddenly, and more than once, in his athletic endeavors and interfered with his ego gratification and his sense of fulfillment (fixed T-Square of ☉ square ♂ on the one side and ♅ conjunct ⊗ on the other); or he displayed tremendous energy (♂ square ☉) and originality (♅) to obtain ego gratification (☉) and fulfillment (⊗). When his talents were used positively he was powerful (☉ trine ♀) and charismatic (☉ trine ♆). If used negatively, however, his personal impression (☉ sesqui-quadrate Ascendant) was less favorable.

Basically his talents flowed when he was disciplined and active before the public (Grand Trine in water: ☿ conjunct ♀ and MC, trine ♄ and trine Ascendant conjunct ☽). His physical energy (☿ conjunct ♀ quintile ♂) could be easily utilized for further development (♀ trine ♃), but if he were confused (☿ square ♆) or exerting power (☿ conjunct ♀ square ♀) the results might not have been so desirable.

EXERCISE 95

Since the co-rulers of the ninth house are in the fifth house (the house of creativity), Babe Ruth's creative talents were reinforced.

Saturn is part of the Grand Trine in water mentioned in Exercise 94, so the ease of his creativity is reiterated. The charisma is restated by Saturn's bi-quintile to Neptune; the possible problems with relationships, by Saturn's sesqui-quadrate to the North Node.

Uranus is part of the fixed T-Square mentioned in Exercise 94. If this T-Square were used positively, Ruth's creativity could grow (♅ bi-quintile ♃), and he could relate easily to others (♅ trine ☊). If used negatively, his emotions could interfere with his abilities (♅ sesqui-quadrate ☽).

EXERCISE 96

Babe Ruth was very active and outgoing in group activities and liked to be where the action was (♈). He would also be persistent and hard-working for group goals and have team loyalty (♉).

He was intiating and aggressive in team efforts (♂ in the eleventh house), and through them his volatility could be directly expressed (fixed T-Square of ♂ opposition ♅ conjunct ⊗, square ☉). If his anger erupted suddenly during a game, this might interfere with his ego gratification (☉) and sense of fulfillment (⊗), as well as present a poor personal impression (♂ semi-square Ascendant). If, however, he directed his great energy (♂ square ☉) creatively (♂ opposition ♅) to express (♂ quintile ♀) his talents (♂ quintile ♀) in his relationships (♂ sextile ☊) and to the world generally (♂ sextile MC), his feeling of accomplishment would be strong (♂ opposition ⊗ and square ☉).

EXERCISE 97

The placement of the ruler of the eleventh house (♂) in the eleventh house emphasizes the importance of group activities.

Since the ruler of the house is in the house, the description of major configurations and aspects would be the same as that given in Exercise 96.

EXERCISE 98

Babe Ruth was more serious and conservative in his close one-to-one relationships and partnerships than in any other area of his life. He had a strong sense of duty and responsibility there. He could provide security for close friends and the partner but needed security from them as well (♑).

EXERCISE 99

He was creative and loving in close friendships, and undoubtedly romantic in marriage (the ruler of the seventh house is in the fifth house).

The volatility which was prevalent in group activities was not evident in close relationships (the fixed T-Square was not connected to either the seventh house or the ruler of the seventh house). Instead he had a strong emotional involvement and was sentimental in close friendships (Grand Trine in water: ♄ trine ♀ conjunct ☿ and MC, and trine Ascendant conjunct ☽). He could easily (Grand Trine) express (☿) his personal (Ascendant) affection (♀) and feelings (☽) to the world (MC). He was sensitive to the needs of those he cared about (♄ bi-quintile ♆), but other relationships (♄ sesqui-quadrate ☊) could sometimes interfere.

SELECTED BIBLIOGRAPHY OF BOOKS EMPHASIZING CHART SYNTHESIS

Dobyns, Zipporah Pottenger and Nancy Roof. *The Astrologer's Casebook*, TIA Publications, Los Angeles, 1973.

Hone, Margaret. *The Modern Text-Book of Astrology*. L.N. Fowler and Co. Ltd., London, 1951.

Lewi, Grant. *Heaven Knows What*. Llewellyn Publications, St. Paul, Minnesota, 1969.

Marks, Tracy. *The Art of Chart Synthesis*. Sagittarius Rising, Natick, Mass., 1979.

Mayo, Jeff. *Teach Yourself Astrology*. Shambala Publications, Inc., Berkely, Cal., 1964.

Negus, Joan. *Basic Astrology: A Guide for Teachers and Students*. Astro Computing Services, San Diego, Cal., 1978.

BIRTH SOURCE INFORMATION

1. Dustin Hoffman: Katherine Clark et al., *Contemporary Sidereal Horoscopes;*, San Francisco: Sidereal Research Publications, 1976.
2. Martin Luther King, Jr.: William Robert Miller, *Martin Luther King, Jr.* New York: Weybright and Talley, Inc., 1968, p.6.
3. Henry Kissinger: *The Mercury Hour,* July, 1975, p.6.
4. Charles Manson: Katherine Clark et al., op. cit.
5. Liza Minnelli: Ibid.
6. Eleanor Roosevelt: Archibald MacLeish, *The Eleanor Roosevelt Story;* Boston: Houghton Mifflin, 1965, p.2.
7. Herman 'Babe' Ruth: Gerald Kissinger, 'Hank Aaron Makes Baseball History', *Horoscope;* May, 1974, p.15.

We calculate...You delineate!

CHART ANALYSIS

Natal Chart wheel with planet/sign glyphs. Choice of house system: Placidus (standard), Equal, Koch, Campanus, Meridian, Porphyry, or Regiomontanus. Choice of tropical (standard) or sidereal zodiac. Aspects, elements planetary nodes, declinations, midpoints, etc 2.00

Arabic Parts All traditional parts and more 1.00

Asteroids Ceres, Pallas, Juno and Vesta. Included in natal wheel + major planet aspects/midpoints .. .50

Astrodynes Power, harmony and discord with summaries for easy comparison 2.00

Chiron, Transpluto or Lilith (only one) in wheel .... N/C

Concentric Wheels Any 3 charts available in wheel format may be combined into concentric wheels 3.00
Deduct $1.00 for each chart ordered as a separate wheel.

Fixed Stars Robson's 110 fixed stars with aspects to natal chart 1.00

Graphic Midpoint Sort Proportional spacing highlights midpt. groupings. **Specify integer divisions of 360°** (1 = 360°, 4 = 90°, etc.) 1.00

Harmonic Chart John Addey-type. Wheel format, harmonic asc eq. houses. **Specify harmonic number** 2.00

Harmonic Positions 30 consecutive sets of positions **Specify starting harmonic number** 1.00

Heliocentric Chart Sun-centered positions 2.00

House Systems Comparison for 7 systems ...... .50

Local Space planet compass directions (azimuth & altitude) plus Campanus Mundoscope .... .50

Locality Map USA or World map showing rise, upper & lower culmination and set lines for each planet . 6.00

Midpoint Structures Midpoint aspects + midpoints in 45° and 90° sequence 1.00

Rectification Assist 10 same-day charts **Specify starting time, time increment, i.e. 6 am, 20 minutes** 10.00

Relocation Chart for current location **Specify original birth data and new location** 2.00

Uranian Planets + half-sums .... .50

Uranian Sensitive Points 3.00

HUMAN RELATIONSHIPS

Chart Comparison (Synastry) All aspects between the two sets of planets plus house positions of one in the other 1.50

Composite Chart Rob Hand-type. Created from midpoints between 2 charts. **Specify location** 2.00

Relationship Chart Chart erected for space-time mid-point between two births 2.00

COLOR CHARTS

4-Color Wheel any chart we offer in new, aesthetic format with color coded aspect lines 2.00

Local Space Map 4-color on 360° circle 2.00

Custom 6" DIAL for any harmonic (laminated, you cut out) overlays on our color wheel charts 4.00

FUTURE TRENDS

Progressed Chart in wheel format. **Specify progressed day, month and year** 2.00

Secondary Progressions Day-by-day progressed aspects to natal and progressed planets, ingresses and parallels by month, day and year. **Specify starting year, MC by solar arc (standard) or RA of mean Sun.** .... 5 years 3.00
10 years 5.00
85 years 15.00

Minor or Tertiary Progressions Minor based on lunar-month-for-a-year, tertiary on day-for-a-lunar-month. **Specify year, MC by solar arc (standard) or RA of mean sun** .... 1 year 2.00

Progressed Lifetime Lunar Phases a la Dane Rudhyar 5.00

Solar Arc Directions Day-by-day solar arc directed aspects to the natal planets, house and sign ingresses by month, day and year. **Specify starting year.** Asc and Vertex arc directions available at same prices .... 1st 5 years 1.00
Each add'l 5 years .50

Primary Arc Directions includes speculum 5 years 1.50 **Specify starting year** ...... Each add'l 5 years .50

Transits by all planets except Moon. Date and time of transiting aspects/ingresses to natal chart. **Specify starting month**. Moon-only transits available at same prices. .... 6 mos. 7.00
12 mos. 12.00
summary only, 6 mos. 3.50
summary only, 12 mos. 6.00

Outer Planet Transits Jupiter thru Pluto 12 mos. .. 3.00

Returns in wheel format. All returns can be precession corrected. **Specify place, Sun-return year, Moon-return month, planet-return month.**
Solar, Lunar or Planet 2.00
13 Lunar 15.00

Custom Graphic Ephemeris in 4 colors. **Specify harmonic, zodiac, starting date.**
1 or 5 YR TRANSITS with or without natal 5.00
1 or 5 YR TRANSITS, NATAL & PROGRESSED .. 7.00
85-YR PROGRESSIONS with natal positions ... 10.00
NATAL LINES ONLY (plus transparency) 4.00
additional natal (same graph) 1.00
additional person's progressions (same graph) . 2.00

POTPOURRI

Custom House Cusps Table For each minute of sidereal time. **Specify latitude ° ' "** 10.00

Custom American Ephemeris Page Any month, 2500BC-2500AD. Specify zodiac (Sidereal includes RA & dec.)
One mo. geocentric or two mos. heliocentric ... 5.00
One year ephemeris (**specify beginning month, year**) 50.00
One year heliocentric ephemeris 25.00

Fertility Chart The Jonas method with Sun/Moon squares/oppositions to the planets, for 1 year. **Specify starting month** 3.00

Lamination of 1 or 2 pages 1.00
Transparency (B/W) of any chart or map 1.00
Handling charge per order 2.00

SAME DAY SERVICE

ASTRO COMPUTING SERVICES
P.O. BOX 16430
SAN DIEGO, CA 92116-0430
NEIL F. MICHELSEN